STRACHEY FAMILY TREE

(For Part II see back endpaper)

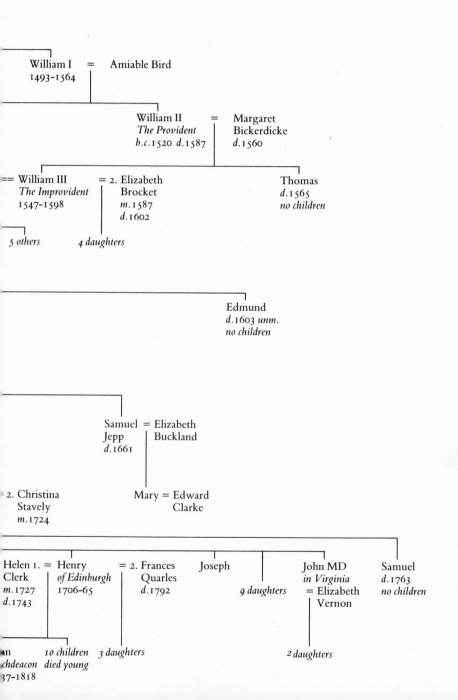

William I = Amiable Bird
1493-1564

William II = Margaret
The Provident Bickerdicke
b.c. 1520 *d.* 1587 *d.* 1560

== William III = 2. Elizabeth   Thomas
The Improvident Brocket   *d.* 1565
1547-1598 *m.* 1587   *no children*
d. 1602

5 others   4 daughters

Edmund
d. 1603 *unm.*
no children

Samuel = Elizabeth
Jepp Buckland
d. 1661

2. Christina   Mary = Edward
Stavely   Clarke
m. 1724

Helen 1. = Henry   = 2. Frances   Joseph   John MD   Samuel
Clerk *of Edinburgh*   Quarles   *in Virginia*   *d.* 1763
m. 1727 1706-65   *d.* 1792   9 daughters   = Elizabeth   *no children*
d. 1743   Vernon

an   10 children 3 daughters   2 daughters
chdeacon died young
37-1818

THE STRACHEY LINE

THE STRACHEY LINE

*An English Family in America, in India
and at home 1570 to 1902*

by

BARBARA STRACHEY

LONDON
VICTOR GOLLANCZ LTD
1985

First published in Great Britain 1985
by Victor Gollancz Ltd,
14 Henrietta Street, London WC2E 8QJ

British Library Cataloguing in Publication Data
Strachey, Barbara
  The Strachey line.
  1. Strachey *(Family)*
  I. Title
  929'.2'0942   CS439.S8978

  ISBN 0-575-03593-5

Photoset in Great Britain by
Rowland Phototypesetting Ltd, Bury St Edmunds, Suffolk
and printed by St Edmundsbury Press
Bury St Edmunds, Suffolk

Contents

List of Illustrations

Richard Strachey in middle age, by William Patten (*Courtesy Lord O'Hagan, Sutton Court. Photo: A. C. Cooper*)

Sir Henry Strachey, 2nd Baronet (1772–1858) by William Patten (*Courtesy Lord O'Hagan, Sutton Court. Photo: A. C. Cooper*)

Following page 96

Richard Strachey (1781–1847). Persian miniature (*Courtesy Lord O'Hagan, Sutton Court. Photo: A. C. Cooper*)

Fath Ali Shah, ruler of Persia in 1800 (*Courtesy India Office Library*)

Khair un Nissa, wife of James Achilles Kirkpatrick (*Courtesy the descendants of Kitty Kirkpatrick*)

James Achilles Kirkpatrick (1764–1805), Artist unknown (*Courtesy Mrs Alladin*)

William Kirkpatrick (1801–28), Artist unknown (*Courtesy Mrs Alladin*)

Nizam Khan Asaf Jah II of Hyderabad (*Courtesy Mrs Alladin*)

The Kirkpatrick children, William and Kitty, by George Chinnery, 1805 (*Courtesy of the Hongkong and Shanghai Bank*)

The Residency at Hyderabad (*Courtesy India Office Library*)

Following page 128

Edward Strachey (1774–1832). Artist unknown (*Courtesy Lord O'Hagan, Sutton Court. Photo courtesy Mary Shaw*)

Julia Kirkpatrick Strachey (1790–1846). Artist unknown (*Courtesy India Office Library*)

Kitty Kirkpatrick (1802–89). From a miniature (*Courtesy the descendants of Kitty Kirkpatrick*)

Thomas Carlyle as a young man (*Courtesy National Portrait Gallery*)

John St Loe Strachey (1860–1926) (*Courtesy Mary Shaw*)

Sir Edward Strachey (1812–1901) and his cat Jim, by his son, Henry Strachey (*Courtesy Lord O'Hagan, Sutton Court. Photo courtesy Mary Shaw*)

Sir John Strachey (1824–1907) (*Courtesy Radio Times Hulton Picture Library*)

Following page 144

Col. Henry Strachey (1816–1912) by Henry Strachey (*Courtesy Royal Geographical Society*)

William Strachey (1819–1904) on the terrace of Sutton Court, 1902

Sir Richard Strachey (1817–1908) as a young man, by M. Yule (*Courtesy India Office Library*)

Jane Maria, Lady Strachey (1840–1928) (*Courtesy National Portrait Gallery*)

Sir Richard Strachey in middle age, by T. Blake Wirgam (*Courtesy India Office Library*)

Sir John (1823–1907) and Sir Richard Strachey, 1876 (*Courtesy National Portrait Gallery*)

Lady Strachey in old age *c.* 1920 (*Author's collection*)

Verse and signature of William Strachey c. 1620 (*Courtesy Princeton University Library*) *page 11*

A map of India showing places mentioned in the Strachey family history *page 12*

Sir Edward Strachey (1812–1901) as a child, with a sister Charlotte who died young (*Courtesy Somerset Record Office*) *page 121*

Two heraldic blazons of Foss the Cat, by Edward Lear (From *Nonsense Songs and Stories*, published by Frederick Warne & Co. Ltd) *page 127*

FAMILY TREES

Verse and signature of William Strachey c. 1620

Ecclesiae et Respub.

Wild as they are accept them, so were we,
To make them civill, will our honour bee
And if good workes be the effectes of mindes
That like good Angells be, let our designes
As we are Angli, make us Angells too
No better work can Church or statesman doe.

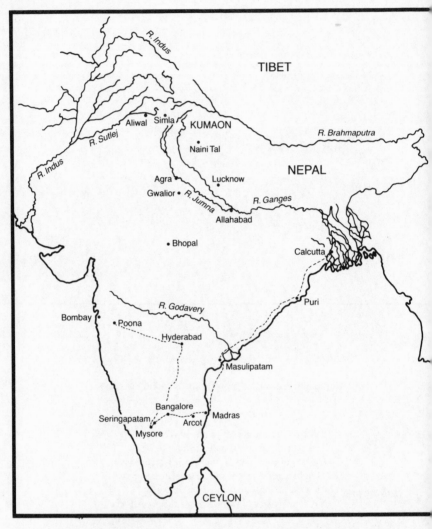

INDIA, showing places mentioned in the Strachey family history

---- marks the journey of Edward Strachey and Mountstuart
Elphinstone from Calcutta to Poona, 1800–1801

Preface

There is necessarily a lot of material to deal with in a chronicle covering three and a half centuries, and I owe my gratitude to a lot of people for helping me to unearth it.

In the first place I must thank Dr C. R. Sanders, whose book *The Strachey Family* (Duke University Press 1953) and the wide research he documented in it, provided invaluable signposts for me.

I must also thank Dr S. G. Culliford, without whose unpublished thesis on William Strachey, the Venturer, for London University, I could not have written my first chapter. Despite all my efforts I have failed to trace him, but London University—to whom I am also most grateful—has given me permission to use his material.

For the manuscript material I have used, much of it unpublished, and for permission to quote from it, I am grateful in the first place to my cousin Charles Strachey, Lord O'Hagan; to the Library of the India Office, where Dr Richard Bingle was extremely helpful; to the Strachey Trust for permission to quote from their material and to Mrs Wilson for helping me with it; to the Somerset Record Office at Taunton; to the William L. Clements Library of the University of Michigan, which has allowed me to consult copies of the Strachey papers in their possession, and to their director, John C. Dann, who made it possible for me to see them; to the New York Public Library for similar permission for their material and also to the descendants of Kitty Kirkpatrick who have most generously allowed me to quote from their papers and to reproduce their photographs.

In India I am particularly grateful to Mrs Bilkiz Alladin, who helped me in Hyderabad, and also to Mr Hurmuz Kaus. I must thank Dr Arleen Shy for advice about the chapter on the

American War of Independence and Katherine Duncan-Jones about that on William the Venturer. Also Jane Havell for constructive criticism, the Raleigh family for hospitality and transport and Lucy Norton for advice and encouragement.

I have been helped in providing the illustrations, also, by many people: my cousin Mary Shaw—who was a godsend—Mrs Miles and Mrs Rohatgi of the India Office Library, Mr Pepper at the Archives of the National Portrait Gallery, Mr Pole of the Saffron Walden Museum, The Royal Geographical Society, The Hongkong and Shanghai Bank, Mrs Bilkiz Alladin, and the descendants of Kitty Kirkpatrick. I am also profoundly grateful to Lord O'Hagan, the owner of Sutton Court, for his kindness in allowing me to photograph there and to reproduce the family portraits. Copyright acknowledgements for all the pictures and details of their whereabouts are to be found in the list of illustrations.

I have added lists of sources and select bibliographies under Chapter headings at the end of the book. Relevant portions of the family tree are to be found in both front and back endpapers and at the beginning of each chapter.

I have not been strictly consistent in the spelling of Indian proper and place names, but have tried to make sure that they are clear for the English-speaking reader. In the chapter on Hyderabad I have kept to the titles of 'Aristojah' and 'Mir Alum', instead of including their names, as the titles are used by Wellington in his letter.

My story ends with the Victorian generation. The Bloomsbury Stracheys and other members of the later generations are part of a very different world, and many of them have already been more than adequately dealt with by others.

February 1985   B.S.

The Yeomen of Saffron Walden

(1450–1600)

Over some ten or eleven generations the Strachey family has tended almost always to produce men of the same character: extremely sceptical, critical, intelligent, scientific, somewhat eccentric, distinctly bad at making money, and having a pronounced taste for literary interests and friends, these last stretching, literally, from Shakespeare to Virginia Woolf. Almost all of them, moreover, have been markedly peaceable, even those few who became soldiers. As the wife of one of the later Stracheys wrote: 'The Stracheys are most strongly the children of their fathers. It does not matter whom they marry, the type continues and has been the same for three hundred years.'

The name does not seem to derive from any place or occupation, and there have never been more than a very few Stracheys at a time, all related to each other.

Efforts have been made to connect the later family with one Sir John Streeche, knighted by the Black Prince in 1337, and his son, Sheriff of Somerset in 1384. It is also thought possible that they are descended from another John Streeche, who kept a court at Oxborough in Norfolk, in the right of his wife, Joan, in 1427. But the first reliable and consecutive records begin to appear in the town of Saffron Walden in Essex, with a yeoman called John Strachey who died around 1460.

Like many other English families the Stracheys rose from yeoman stock in the sixteenth century, accepted the reformed religion without demur, and a century later acquired a smallish manor house which is still in the possession of their descendants today.

Stracheys were among the first Englishmen to set foot in America, and one of them took an important part in negotiating the Peace Treaty after the American War of Independence. In the eighteenth century, again like other impecunious country gentry, they found their way to India, where they served for four generations.

Their connection with India started with Clive and lasted until the First World War, through the days of the Wellesley brothers and Tippoo Sultan, of the far-off struggle with the French, the final disintegration of the Mogul Empire, through times of widespread corruption and early death, and the reluctant transformation of a faraway trading concession into what was, perhaps, the strangest empire of them all.

Almost all the thirteen Stracheys who went to India served there with distinction, but without achieving the wealth commonly attributed to the Nabobs, or wishing to; loving the country, the culture and the people and exercising their talents and their scientific curiosity in many fruitful ways.

It is largely this relationship with India that I wish to chronicle, but before I can reach it I must describe what went before.

The middle of the sixteenth century was one of the great turning points of English history. Henry VIII's matrimonial obstinacy opened the door to the religious Reformation, but other almost equally important changes were stirring.

The expansion of the art of printing led not only to the great literary Renaissance but also to a widening and humanization of the constrictive theological education of the Middle Ages. Foreign trade was increasing, both in the Levant, where the Venetian monopoly had at last come to an end, and further afield, with the wide-ranging enterprises of the Merchant Venturers. Land was changing hands throughout the country, and more was involved than the confiscated church lands. Tenant farmers were getting richer and buying freehold estates, and landlords were getting poorer as inflation reduced the value of their rents. The poorest people—as always—were yet further crushed, but the middle class of yeomen, the free tenants, or franklins, profited enormously, and the rise of the new 'gentry' drawn from this class, was one of the most prominent features of the age.

These changes were all more evident in the areas round London, and East Anglia had always had the highest proportion of free tenants in the country and had further benefited from its geographical situation, facing Flanders, the traditional market for English wool.

The little town of Walden—Saffron Walden as it was called—became known throughout Europe for the quality of the saffron (a valuable dye and medicinal herb) which was grown in its fields. It lay some 35 to 40 miles north of London, and had the additional advantage of an absentee Lord of the Manor, and was thus able to run its affairs unmolested.

The town had been a prosperous settlement from the time of the Romans, and by 1500 it consisted of some 200–300 households. Among the three or four principal families were the Stracheys, civic-minded tradesmen and yeomen, a number of whose activities had been recorded there since around 1450. The clan was a large one at that time, and included sheep farmers, drapers, butchers and alehouse keepers as well as the head of the nearby Abbey at Pleshey and a Bailiff of the county town, Colchester. Throughout the century the family became gradually more prosperous until by 1570 one William Strachey, a particularly shrewd man and a great grandson of the John Strachey who had died around 1460, was by far the wealthiest man in Saffron Walden.

The transformation of the tenant farmers into gentry was now going ahead fast. Profits were being made from trade as well as agriculture and more and more men began to apply for the right to bear arms to confirm their claims to be gentlemen. Such arms were granted freely, moreover, for a suitable fee, to anyone who could show that he was living 'in the style of a gentleman', a typically vague English classification, and that he had enough money to support this way of life. Old-fashioned characters tended to find the process of buying arms snobbish and distasteful, and very likely William Strachey, although he clearly considered himself a gentleman, did not choose to apply on his own account. Sons, however, could apply on behalf of their fathers and thus at one stroke acquire—as Shakespeare did in 1596—the status of second-generation gentleman. It may well be, therefore, that the arms granted to William in 1587, a few months after his death, were applied for by his son, another William who was a much less worthy character than his father.

This William was born in 1547 and educated at the ambitious new Saffron Walden school, founded by the city fathers 'to teach grammar within the town after the form of Winchester or of Eton'. It had a high reputation and was run by a Cambridge Master of Arts, 'a profound grammarian'. Following this young William was enrolled in the Middle Temple, a common practice at that time for young men not necessarily intending to become lawyers but seeking cultural and metropolitan polish.

There, in 1566, he made the acquaintance of a fellow student called Richard Cooke, scion of rich merchant stock. Richard had a younger sister, Mary, and three years later William married her and settled in London. Father William, however, summoned his son home, with his wife and three young children, in 1574, though probably neither William nor Mary was overjoyed at the move. Mary was a stranger in a small town, and young William never took the interest his father did in Walden's civic affairs. There was a considerable inheritance involved, however, and when father William died in 1587, he left 13 houses, more than 200 acres of freehold arable land and pasture in Walden and Wimbush, 100 more of copyhold land, three houses and a cottage leased from Walden Manor, and a Brewhouse in St Margaret's Westminster, a property consisting of five dwellings, three stables, a garden and a wharf.

Young William's wife, Mary, died within a month of his father's death, and he married again somewhat precipitately, in fact within three months. By this time his eldest son, yet another William (the Venturer) was fifteen years old and the following year he was sent to Cambridge, to the newly founded Puritan college, Emmanuel. Following his father's example he then enrolled at Gray's Inn, the largest and most influential of the Inns of Court.

In his choice of a bride, Frances Forster, he followed his father's example too, for she was the daughter of a wealthy merchant of Camberwell who was later knighted.

William lived with the Forster family until his own father died in 1598 leaving a further four children by his second wife. At this point the young man, now 26, had to return to Saffron Walden to clear up the estate, which was a good deal smaller than the one his father had inherited only ten years earlier. This time the inheritance was, in fact, a considerable embarrassment. Everything was left to the widow, Elizabeth, for her life, and only then to young William, who found himself having to support four small half-sisters, pay an annuity to one brother, lend £200 to another and rescue a defaulting brother-in-law from the clutches of a notorious money-lender. His stepmother married again almost at once, however, and an amicable lawsuit enabled him to sell some of the property for his own benefit, while two years later her death released him from Saffron Walden, with Frances and his little son, to go and live with his in-laws on their estate at Crowhurst in Surrey.

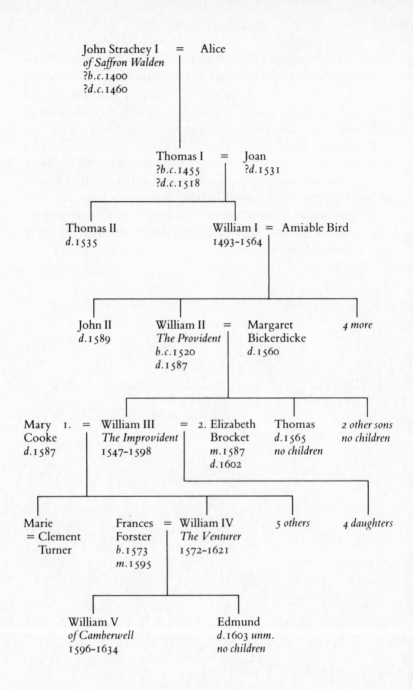

FAMILY TREE I

THE MERCHANT VENTURER

William Strachey

(1572–1621)

During the two plague years, 1602 and 1603, William Strachey was probably happy to stay on at Crowhurst, and his second son, Edmund, was born there in 1603. By the following year, however, he had acquired bachelor lodgings at Blackfriars, and was taking his first steps in the stirring literary world of London.

He already almost certainly had one acquaintance in that world in the person of Gabriel Harvey, close friend of Spenser, who also hailed from Saffron Walden. Harvey was about the same age as William and of the same rising social class, and clearly knew his family. In his Marginalia, written about 1598, is the entry, '"Lay your cares in a narrow room": Mrs Strachey to her husband.'

The next friend whom he found to ally himself with was Francis Michell, another Essex man, but some twenty years older. Michell's was a very variegated career; he was imprisoned at one stage in Rome, knighted, admitted bribery, was degraded from his knighthood and was sent to the Tower by Parliament but released by the King. The enterprise upon which he was now engaged was the publication of a pirated travel book called *A View of Fraunce*.

William wrote commendatory verses for this rather dubious work in 1604, a form of publicity for both author and versifier which was common at the time, and which served, perhaps, the same purpose as a favourable review today.

The following year William wrote more commendatory verses (and it must be admitted very bad ones) for the publication of the Quarto edition of Ben Jonson's play, *Sejanus*, as did his friends George Chapman, Hugh Holland, John Marston and several others. William's verse took the form of a sonnet of high, if obscure, moral tone.

How high a Poore man shows in low estate
Whose base is firme and whole Frame competent,
That sees his cedar made the shrub of fate:
Th'one's little, lasting; th'other's confluence spent.
And as the Lightning comes behind the Thunder
From the torne cloud, yet first invades our Sense;
So every violent Fortune, that to wonder
Hoists men aloft, is a clear evidence
Of a vaunt-courring blow the Fates have given
To his first state: swift Lightning blinds his eyes,
While Thunder, from comparison-hating Heaven
Dischargeth on his height, and there it lyes!
If men would shun swoll'n Fortune's ruinous blasts
Let them use temperance; nothing violent lasts.

Shakespeare was of course a friend of Jonson, and both Shakespeare and Burbage had acted in *Sejanus* in 1603.

William soon made other friends in the literary and dramatic world. It was a small world, probably comprising not more than a hundred or two hundred people. Many of William's friends were also friends of Shakespeare, such as Hugh Holland, Richard Martin and John Donne, and although there is no evidence for it, it is very likely that the two Williams were acquainted.

There were two sorts of theatre by the time James I came to the throne in 1603, 'public' and 'private'. The public theatres were 'Big O's', like Shakespeare's Globe across the river from Blackfriars, where the audience sat in the open air, performances were held in daylight and the prices were set low to pull in the man in the street. The merchants and leading citizens of London, however, were strongly Puritan in their views, and forbade such theatres to operate within the walls of the city.

'Private theatres' for the most part operated not in places built specifically for entertainment, but in Great Halls of Inns of Court, Colleges or noble houses. Here the performances could be held indoors, by candlelight; the audience consisted of students, courtiers, or professional men, and the prices were considerably higher.

The best known of the impresarios of the time, Shakespeare's partner, Richard Burbage, had taken a lease of the dining hall at Blackfriars, an old convent building half in and half out of the City, by the river, on a lane which is still called Playhouse Yard. Burbage had hoped to be able to use this as a public theatre, as the building still held Sanctuary rights and did not fall within the jurisdiction of the City, but the inhabitants protested strongly, and he was forced to lease it to a Welshman called Evans and transfer himself and his company, the King's Men, across the river to the Globe instead.

Evans, by joining forces with the Singing Boys of the Chapel Royal, managed to open a private theatre in Blackfriars. It did not take him long to make a considerable success; the music and the acting were both excellent, and his enterprise offered severe competition to the Globe, provoking Shakespeare's wry comment in *Hamlet*:

'There is, Sir, an aerie of children, little eyases, that cry out on the top of the question and are most tyrannically clapped for't. These are now the fashion and so berattle the common stages— so they call them—that many wearing rapiers are afraid of goose quills and dare scarcely come hither.'

In addition to his company of actors, which included the gifted boys, or 'eyases' as Shakespeare called them, Evans had collected a brilliant and sophisticated team of playwrights, headed by Ben Jonson, which included among others Thomas Dekker, George Chapman and John Marston. The last of these was one of the most irreverent, licentious and hot-tempered of all the rowdy literary characters of the day—until he had a change of heart, and was ordained a clergyman.

It was among these men, and other writers such as John Donne, Hugh Holland and Thomas Campion, that William made his friends and passed his drinking hours. Campion, for instance, who was given to writing Latin verses, dedicated one to Guglielmus Strachaeum, describing him as an old boon companion, and crediting him with composing many elegant little verses and being an energetic champion of the Muses. It was perhaps not surprising that by 1605 William had mortgaged all his Saffron Walden property and was desperate for some other kind of income.

Queen Elizabeth, in her day, had relieved Blackfriars of what was normally the greatest running expense of a theatre, by providing all their costumes free, but James did not continue this privilege and Evans, who was not the soundest of operators began to run into trouble.

One of the methods the Chapel Royal was entitled to use in recruiting boys with good voices for the Choir was 'impressing' them. Evans extended this practice for his own purposes at Blackfriars to cover the acting boys, and made the mistake of taking up the son of a Norfolk gentleman of strong Puritanical opinions, who not only sued him but took the matter to the Star Chamber Court in an effort to have the whole 'vile' business of acting abolished. In this he did not succeed—too many powerful men at Court enjoyed the drama—but it became desirable for Evans himself to take a less prominent part in the management of his theatre. He first deeded ownership to his wife and son-in-law, keeping half the profits to himself as 'employed manager', and then drew in a number of what were called 'housekeepers' or shareholders, to act as buffers against authority. Of these William Strachey became one, holding a sixth share. The only other theatre, incidentally, where ownership was shared in this way was the Globe, where Shakespeare, too, was a 'housekeeper'.

Blackfriars soon ran into more trouble. A play called *Eastward Ho*, satirizing James Stuart's 'uncouth' Scottish followers, caused offence when it was performed in 1604. The joint authors were Jonson, Chapman and Marston, and Chapman and Marston were briefly sent to Bridewell prison, while Jonson (whose part in it was very small) voluntarily followed them. The matter however did not take long to blow over and they were soon released. A few years later Chapman went too far again. He wrote a satirical play called *Charles Duke of Biron*, produced in 1608, which drew a violent protest from the French ambassador. The King's displeasure, combined with the fact that 1608 was another plague year, forced Evans out, and after moving for a time to Whitefriars, the company eventually split up.

For a time before the blow fell, William had been making some profit out of the business, calling at the theatre two or three times a week, as he himself recorded, to collect his share of the takings.

A curious mystery emerges at this period. In Shakespeare's *Twelfth Night* there is a sentence which has never been satisfactorily explained. Malvolio, seeking precedents for his impudence in aspiring to the hand of his mistress, says: 'There is example for't: the lady of the Strachy married the yeoman of the wardrobe.' (II.v.39–40). Any number of explanations have been offered by scholars for this remark: that 'the Strachy' was a 'Stratarch'—a general, an oriental Satrapy, the Italian Strozzi family, an expert in stitchery or in starching ruffs, or other far-fetched notions. We have learned, however, from the recently discovered record of a lawsuit in 1606 in which both men were witnesses, that the Wardrobe master of Blackfriars theatre at the time when Strachey was a shareholder was in fact an illiterate tailor called David Yeomans.

It is immensely tempting to believe that this solves the question, but there are still many mysteries involved.

In the first place if the reference does refer to William Strachey it cannot have been included in the original prompt book, as the play was first performed early in 1602, before William came to Blackfriars, whereas the First Folio, which does contain the reference, was not published until 1623. It is not clear, either, who the 'Lady of the Strachy' could have been. William's first wife, Frances, apparently did not live in his Blackfriars lodging and died before him, in 1615. Dorothy, his second wife, probably survived his death in 1621, but had she then married Yeomans it would have been many years after the association with Strachey had ended and the Blackfriars company had been dispersed.

It is conceivable that one of William's young half-sisters was the lady mentioned, two of them would have been of marriageable age by 1606, but there is no trace of such a marriage. Possibly 'marry' was an exaggeration, and Yeomans stole a mistress from Strachey and this became known in the theatre world and used as a gag by the actors at the Globe. The coincidence seems too great for there not to have been some connection. But from what we can gather, such a jibe would have been uncharacteristic of

Shakespeare himself, and the question must, alas, be left un-answered.

In 1606 Strachey's profits from the theatre were already falling off, and he was forced to try another expedient to escape the bailiffs. The current Ambassador to the court of the Sultan of Turkey was Henry Lello, a mild and learned man who had not shown up too well in the complicated and corrupt world of the Seraglio. His secretary, Thomas Glover, came back to England determined to replace him, and contrived to get himself appointed to the post. Strachey was an educated man with a clear and elegant handwriting (as we know from a manuscript of his now in the possession of the Library of Princeton University) and he also had a cousin, John Strachey, who was a prosperous merchant in the Levant trade and who may have recommended him. In any case, William offered his services, was appointed as Glover's secretary, and sailed with him for Constantinople in the late summer of 1606.

Unfortunately Glover turned out to be a thoroughly disagree-able man, not too scrupulous and possessed of an uncontrollable temper. When he was still in office Lello had protested to his employer, Salisbury, in London about his secretary's behaviour, and while awaiting his reply had moved into the house next door to the Embassy, where Glover found him on his arrival—much to his fury. Glover was even angrier when he discovered that most of his staff, including Strachey and his friend, Hugh Holland, who had joined Glover's party on his way out, pre-ferred Lello's company to his and spent all their free time next door with him. Finally he became so incensed that he burst into William's room in the middle of the night, accused him of treason, and dismissed him on the spot.

Certainly both William and Holland had been unwisely open about their friendship for Lello. Holland was a wild and extrava-gant fellow, not one to smooth things over or be tactful. Lello wrote home in Strachey's defence and Salisbury in London, who had clearly recognized by then that the fault was likely to have been at least in part Glover's, sent a mild reply, but though Lello was later given a knighthood nothing was done to reinstate Strachey, and he was forced to sail for home.

William did not reach England for nearly a year. It is possible that he came home by way of Venice, for he made an effort to get another post there, and his good friend, John Donne, wrote a letter of recommendation for him to the Ambassador, Sir Henry Wotton. After claiming friendship with William, Donne reported that 'he had been sometime secretary to Sir Thomas Glover' and added, 'I do boldly say that the greatest folly he ever committed was to submit himself and parts to so mean a master.' No post was, however, forthcoming.

In 1606 a Charter had been granted to the Virginia Company of London to resettle the colony there. Two previous expeditions had been total failures, but now a new one was sent out, in December 1606, under Captain John Smith, and a fort was built at James Town. In 1609 a further expedition with some 500 to 900 settlers was to follow, led by Sir Thomas Gates as the new Deputy Governor, with a fleet of six ships under their admiral, Sir George Somers.

Strachey consulted with his friends Donne and Richard Martin, both of whom were enthusiastic, and finally bought two shares in the Company at £12. 10s. each—perhaps financed by his in-laws or his mother's family—and decided to venture in person.

Both Somers and Gates sailed in the flagship of the little fleet, *The Sea Adventurer*, and Strachey too was on board. In July, as they reached the Caribbean, they met the tail-end of a hurricane. The ships were forced to separate, but all except *The Sea Adventurer* met again after the storm and made their way on to Virginia. *The Sea Adventurer*, however, was less fortunate, and Strachey later told in detail what befell them.

There were disastrous leaks, and they were forced to throw overboard all the ordnance and 'many a barrel of beer, hogshead of oil, cider and wine etc'. They also jettisoned all the personal luggage ('in which I suffered no mean loss,' noted Strachey). The water still rose, however, and they all—including Gates and Somers—had to man the pumps, which at one stage were choked with biscuit, for three days and four nights. Strachey's description is vivid and straightforward. 'There might be seen', he says, 'master, master's mate, boatswain, coopers, carpenters and who not, with candles in their hands, creeping along the ribs viewing the sides searching every corner and listening in every place if they could hear the water run. Many a weeping leak was this way found and hastily stopped, and at length one in the gunner room made up with I know not how many pieces of beef.'

At one stage he describes the apparition of St Elmo's Fire: 'A little round light like a faint star trembling and streaming along with a sparkling blaze, half the height upon the main mast . . . for three or four hours together, or rather more than half the night it kept with us, running sometimes along the Main Yard to the very end and then returning.' They had almost given up hope when at last land was sighted—Bermuda—and in a miraculous calm they were able to run the ship ashore and wedge her between two rocks so that she didn't sink and they were able to salvage the invaluable tools and implements.

There were 150 souls on board, 140 men and 10 women and children, and not one was lost. But their adventures were only just beginning.

They were not the first to be shipwrecked on these islands, and the Venturers found Spanish coins in the sand and numerous hogs in the woods. The island was uninhabited and had acquired the ominous name of 'Isle of Devils', but to them it was entirely benevolent. They stayed there for nine months and found ample food of all kinds, fishes, lobsters, turtles, many kinds of birds, including one they called 'bat-owls' and fruits. They even planted English seeds such as lettuces, and a number of these duly sprouted but were eaten by pests.

In the event both Gates and Somers proved to be admirable leaders. The mate and six sailors were first despatched in the ship's longboat to seek help, but they met with some disaster and failed to reappear, so work was started on building ships capable of carrying them all to Virginia.

Strachey is modest and observant in telling the tale of those nine months, and his detail is always lively and to the point. There were many instances of deliberate idleness and a number of revolts and mutinies which Gates and Somers put down firmly but without harshness. Four men were banished for a time to an uninhabited islet and later pardoned; one man, Stephen Hopkins, was clearly a communistic 'Leveller' or 'Brownist', much addicted to misquoting the Scriptures. He, too, was pardoned when Strachey himself among others spoke for him. He eventually returned to England only to set sail again, for New England this time, seeking more congenial fellow-colonists.

Another rebel, one Thomas Paine, was sentenced to be hanged, but being a gentleman begged to be shot instead, and as Strachey reports, 'Towards evening he had his desire, the sunne and his life setting together.'

They built two ships of green cedar wood—a considerable feat—and finally reached the mouth of the James river, where: 'we had a marvellous sweet smell from the shore—strong and pleasant, which did not a little glad us.'

Strachey says practically nothing of his own part in all this, except to note that he was godfather to one of the two children born on the island, a girl named Bermuda Rose, but it is clear that he worked hard and loyally in difficult circumstances.

On their arrival in Virginia they found the settlement in a disastrous condition, besieged by Indians and reduced from 900 to 60 by plague, starvation and incompetence.

Strachey continues his tale with a critical description of the state of affairs, claiming that Virginia was a highly fertile country with a benevolent climate and that the settlers themselves were to blame for their disasters. The fort had been built in the wrong place—too low and 'feverish'—and where there were no fresh springs, only a brackish well; mutiny, bad leadership and idleness, he claimed, were to blame for the chaos. 'Unto such a calamity,' he said, 'can sloath, riot and vanity bring the most settled and plentiful estate.'

Despite Gates's best efforts matters had gone too far, and he was forced to order the settlement to be abandoned. On their way down the river, however, they were providentially met by the new Governor, himself, Lord De la Warr, who was taking over from his deputy, Gates, and bringing plentiful fresh supplies, and they were able to turn back.

Clearly Strachey's honesty, energy and enthusiasm were highly regarded by the leaders, for he was given the important post of Secretary of the Colony, and for the next year was in a position of considerable authority and in close communication with the Company's Council in England. Gates, who returned to London in July 1610, took with him an official report and also Strachey's personal detailed description of the wreck, which he called 'A True Reportory of the Wracke and Redemption of Sir Thomas Gates upon and from the Islands of the Bermudas'.

Meanwhile one of his friends, Richard Martin, had become Secretary of the Company in London, and he wrote to William in December of that year praising his work and asking for a further report on the Colony. 'I must crave your pardon,' he wrote, 'if considering many present impediments I wrap up a great desire of advertisement and good affection in few words, my desire is chiefly to let you understand how well your travail in that place where you are is interpreted among all good and wise men, which having been still in love with long and hazardous voyages, more to profytt your knowledge than for any other profytt, showes that you have a mynde much in love with virtue.'

Ignoring the somewhat ominous absence of any practical promises, Strachey therefore started making notes and observations for such a report, but in 1611 Gates came out to James Town again and Strachey was recalled. He arrived home in the autumn of 1611, expecting to be given some rewarding new post, but nothing whatever was done for him. As he was to write later in his Commonplace book: 'The world's promises are only fayre, nothing so in performance. It is as Laban's words to Jacob, a promise of the beautiful Rachel if we will serve it, but performs unto us bleered-eyed Leah.'

The reason for this neglect was almost certainly his very honesty and frankness. The Virginia Company was desperately anxious to avoid discouraging new settlers and to attract more capital, and despite Strachey's encouraging praise of the land itself, his remarks about 'sloath' and 'vanity' were not at all what they wanted.

'The True Reportory,' his letter about the storm, was suppressed and not published until 1625, after Strachey's death and the dissolution of the Company.

Meanwhile, however, it had been privately circulated among Council members and their friends, and no doubt talked about.

During late 1610 and early 1611, just at the time when the account arrived, Shakespeare started to write his last great play, *The Tempest*. He undoubtedly saw not only the official report of the Company, including a brief description of the storm by a man called Sylvester Jourdain, which had been authorized by the Council and made public, but also Strachey's 'True Reportory'. It has been demonstrated that he could have had full access to this probably through influential friends in the Council, and that it was, indeed, his main source for the tempest he described in his play. The derivations are many and exact, with impressive verbal correspondences as well as borrowings of such details as the St Elmo's Fire which Ariel caused to flame on the topmast, the deep nook in the 'still vex'd Bermoothes' where the King's ship was hidden, the birds caught on the rocks, a drink made of berries, Gonzalo's mock praise of communism, the mention of 'bat-fowling', the butts of wine heaved overboard—even the 'sloth' and 'standing water' of the colony.*

The Tempest was first performed at Whitehall on 1st November 1611, soon after Strachey arrived back at his Blackfriars lodgings. He had almost certainly been acquainted with Shakespeare before, but even if he had not, one surely cannot doubt that they met now.

Failing to publish his 'True Reportory', Strachey now turned his energies to the description of Virginia, with its natural characteristics and the people who inhabited it, which he had been asked to provide. His notes are thrown together rather haphazardly, since he was in a hurry to get them out, but they show an impartial and scientific interest in what he saw and heard, and particularly in the Indians. He assembled a respectable phonetic vocabulary of their language which has proved valuable to modern scholars of Indian linguistics; he explored their religion, their philosophy of life and death and their social habits. He took a benevolently imperialistic view of them, demanding that they should be fairly treated, and convinced that they would

---

* A full record of all these correspondences together with much of Strachey's text can be found in Bullough's *Narrative and Dramatic sources of Shakespeare*, Vol. VIII, 1975.

benefit by being converted to Christianity. Of their impressive Chief, Powhatan, he said:

> He is a goodly old man, not yet shrinking, though well beaten with many cold and stormy winters. He is supposed to be a little less than 80 years old. He has been a strong and able salvage, synovie active and of a daring spirit. Cruell he hath been and quarrellous, and sure it is to be wondered at how such a barbarous and uncivill Prynce should take unto him such a Majestie as he expresseth, which oftentimes strykes awe and sufficient wonder into our people.

He describes Powhatan's daughter, Pocahontas, as a 'well featured but wanton young girl sometimes resorting to our fort, of the age of 11 or 12 years. [She would] gett the boyes forth with her into the market place and make them wheele falling on their hands turning their heels upwards, whome she would follow and wheele so herself, naked as she was.'

He adds that Pocahontas was later married to a private Captain called Koucum. It seems likely that 'Pocahontas' was not a proper name, but a title or term of affection, and that more than one of Powhatan's daughters were called by it. John Smith's well-known story of how she saved him from her father was very probably an invention, and was set some years earlier, when this girl would have been a mere child. There was, however, certainly one historical character of that name, who married John Rolfe, became a Christian and went with him to London where she was received by King James and his Queen. This Pocahontas took the name of Rebecca, had her portrait painted and died and was buried in England.

Strachey had no luck with this book, either. John Smith, the previous governor, wishing to justify himself, had rushed into print with a collection consisting of various pieces by himself and others which was called *A Map of Virginia*. It was published early in 1612 and killed Strachey's project stone dead. He hurriedly assembled his notes and entitled them '*A History of Travaile in Virginia Britania*', but the Council was not now interested. Once

The Close (on the corner of High Street and Castle Street, Saffron Walden),
home of William Strachey, the Venturer, until 1600

Sutton Court. Engraving by J. Collinson for his book, *History of Somerset*,
1792, after a drawing by one of Clive's daughters

The first Booke
of
the first Decade,

Conteyning the Historie of travell into Virginia Britania, expressing the Cosmographie, & Commodi:ties of the Countrie, together with the Qualities, Customes, and Manners of the naturall Inhabitants.

in part gathered and obseyned from the industrious and faithfull Observations, and Commentaries of the first Planters & elder Discouerers, and in parte observed by **William Strachey** gent, three yeeres thether imployed, & sometyme Secretary, & of Counsaile with the most hono.ble the Lord **Lawarre** his Ma.ties Lord Gouernour, and Captaine Generall, for the Collonie.

—— Nec sermones ego mallem

Repentes per humum, quam res componere gestas,
Terrarumqz situs, et Flumina dicere, et aries
Montibus impositas, et barbara regna — Hor: Ep: lib. 2. Ep. 1.

First page of William Strachey's manuscript, *A History of Travaile in Virginia Britania*, c. 1612, in the author's own hand again it contained too much frank detail for them, and no one could be found to act as patron for him. In increasing despondency Strachey applied first to the Earl of Northumberland, friend of Raleigh, who was then in easy confinement in the Tower. Failing a response he tried Apsley, Purveyor of His Majesty's Navy, but still without success.

The threat of a debtor's prison was again looming. The bailiffs descended on him and he wrote to an unidentified friend:

> Sir. Necessities, not my will, sendes me unto you a borrower of 20s if you may; this last dismal arrest hath taken from all my friends something and from me all I had; and today I am to meete with some friends at dinner returned from Virginia, and God is witness with me I have not to pay for my dinner. All my things be at pawn and I yet indebted.

He was harried by lawsuits, among others one concerning the brewhouse he had inherited, and beset by troubles of all kinds, and in 1618, with a last desperate effort he sent the third copy of the manuscript of his '*Travaile*' to Francis Bacon, offering to dedicate it to him. He received no reply, and the work was not, in fact, published until 1849.

Meanwhile his wife Frances had died. She seems not to have come with him to London, but probably stayed at Crowhurst with their two sons. How often William returned there we do not know. After Frances's death he married again and went to live in Camberwell, where he died, but nothing is known of his second wife except that her name was Dorothy and that she was a widow.

Unlike later Stracheys his troubles had turned his thoughts to religion and penitence, and in his last years he filled a Commonplace Book (now in the possession of the University of Virginia) with comments on Church history and doctrine and heartfelt protestations of sorrow for his riotous youth. He even composed a sermon. Some verses also survive in the Bodleian at Oxford, described in a contemporary hand as '*Mr Strachey's Hark*'.

Harke! Twas the trump of death that blows.
My hower is come false world adewe.
Thy pleasures have betrayed me soe
That I to death untimely goe.
For Death's the punishment of sinn
And of all creatures I have bene
The most ungrateful wicked one
That ere the heavens did shine upon.

He died in 1621, aged 49. He left no Will; indeed he had nothing to leave as he had already deeded the troublesome brewhouse to his elder son.

Strachey was a frustrated and disappointed man, in spite of possessing excellent abilities which were recognized by his contemporaries. He was—largely not through his own fault—something of a failure in life, but he has not been forgotten, for he provided the 'bones' which a greater man transformed into 'Something rich and strange'.

SUTTON COURT

From William of Camberwell to Henry of Edinburgh

(1621–1764)

The Venturer's son, William IV (of Camberwell) was not distinguished for anything except marrying, which he did three times, in spite of only living to be 38—and for retrieving the family fortunes in the process.

One of his sons by his first wife followed his grandfather's example and went out to Virginia, where he married and had a daughter, Arabella. But it was his third wife who was the important one. She was Elizabeth Cross, of an old and distinguished Somerset family. Her uncle, Robert Cross, had been one of Queen Elizabeth's most valued sailors, with Sir Richard Grenville at Flores of the Azores and knighted for his part in the siege of Cadiz in 1596.

Elizabeth Cross was already the widow of a London merchant called Jepp when she married William. She had two sons, Samuel Jepp and John, son of William Strachey. When William died in 1635, Elizabeth was still young, and returned with her children to her native Somerset and there married for a third time, Edward Baber, member of a well born and well-to-do family there.

Baber had taken a lease of a smallish fortified manor called Sutton Court, some 15 miles south of Bristol, near Chew Magna; an old stone house with a round Norman tower, surrounded by a battlemented wall and with avenues of elms and limes. The oldest part probably dated from the twelfth century, and in the mid-1400s it was acquired by a family of Norman origin called St Loe, who added a manor house to the old tower.

An early St Loe, John, who built the battlemented wall, was, we are told, a giant: certainly an effigy of him seven foot four inches in height and two foot four inches across the shoulders still lies in Chew Magna church. 'While he was nimbly placing the large stones in place', reports a later Strachey, 'a neighbour, also a

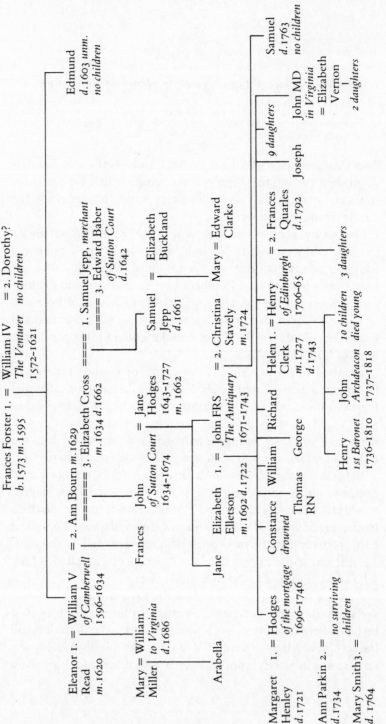

FAMILY TREE 2

giant, called De Hauteville and known as the terror of the inhabitants of Norton, came by and asked why he was making the wall. St Loe replied: "To keep out such fellows as you". Whereupon de Hauteville immediately stepped over the wall.' Sir John Hauteville also has a huge effigy, carved out of a solid piece of Irish oak, which was moved to Chew Magna church when his own was destroyed.

The giant's grandson, Sir William St Loe, was Captain of Queen Elizabeth's Yeoman Guards, and Chief Butler of England, and was the third husband of the celebrated Bess of Hardwick—Building Bess, as she was called—who, as her name implies, could not resist improving and adding to any house she could lay her hands on. She certainly improved and enlarged Sutton Court. She had four husbands in all: the first died before the marriage was consummated; by the second, Sir William Cavendish, she had six children, and then married Sir William St Loe, and though they had no children, St Loe disinherited his own two daughters by a previous marriage and left the manor to Bess's son Charles Cavendish whose son was later created Earl of Newcastle by Charles I. At this point Sutton Court was leased to Edward Baber, and at his death his widow, Elizabeth, bought the estate outright. As her eldest son, Samuel Jepp, died before she did, she left it to her second son, John Strachey, and since then it has remained in the Strachey family.

All this left the family in a much more advantageous position, both financially and socially. They were now landed gentry occupying their time in looking after their property and their tenants, shooting, fishing, and acting as local Justices of the Peace, and enjoying all the other typical avocations of their kind through the centuries.

John, however, was no country clod. He appears to have been handsome, a little lazy, perhaps, but a shrewd, intelligent and educated man. His best friend from childhood was the philosopher and scientist John Locke, author of the *Essay on Human Understanding*, considered one of the greatest of modern philosophers.

Locke was born in the next village; he was two years older than Strachey, knew him as a child, went to school and University with him, and remained virtually a member of the family until John died in 1674, and indeed afterwards.

Such a friendship was no sinecure. The two men corresponded frequently and discussed politics and philosophy, economics, books and science, as well as exchanging personal news and stories to laugh at. Locke's letters are voluble and friendly as well as frequent, while Strachey, being, like so many of his family, addicted to puzzles, tended to amuse himself by wrapping up his meaning in a cryptic form. As Locke once complained to him: 'I wonder what made you twist your lines into whipcord thus, with such a knot at the end of it that I must confess I cannot untie, indeed your letter is like an epigram in prose, good all over with a sting in the tail.'

John Strachey, born in 1634, was only a child at the outbreak of the Civil War, and his father already dead. Despite their nearness to the much fought-over city of Bristol, therefore, the Stracheys were able to keep out of all the fighting, and while they were certainly Parliamentarian in their sympathies, they were not bigoted. John went up to London to see the Restoration of Charles II in 1660, and one can see from his portrait with its long hair and lace collar, that he was no 'Canting Puritan'. Indeed he appears to have been—as so many Stracheys have been through the generations—a complete sceptic.

Locke was somewhat more religious, though he was profoundly tolerant and told John that he preferred 'goodnatured Catholics to stern Puritans'. His father had intended him for the ministry and his college was reluctant to continue the grant he enjoyed unless he took orders. So he asked around for the advice of his friends. When he asked Strachey, he got an uncompromising reply. 'I have always looked on you', John wrote, 'as one of a higher head than to take covert under a cottage, and in my opinion the best country parsonage is no more, and although our holy mother makes better provision for some of her children and bestows letters and preferments on them, yet the expectation is so tedious and the observance so base besides the uncertainty, that it will tire the patience of an ingenious spirit to wait upon such an old doting grandame.'

Locke was a widely cultured man, both in classical and in

scientific studies, though never, it appears, very gifted at mathematics, which was always the Strachey speciality. He was modest and objective, and became one of the first Fellows of the new Royal Society. In 1665 he was sent on a diplomatic mission to Germany, whence he wrote frequent long letters to John.

On his return he was offered a further diplomatic post in Spain, but turned it down as he wished to stay in Oxford and study medicine. 'Those fair offers I had to go to Spain', he wrote to John, 'have not prevailed with me. Whether fate or fondness kept me at home I know not; whether I have let slip the moment that they say everyone has once in his life to make himself I cannot tell; this I am sure, I never trouble myself for the loss of that which I never had; and I have the satisfaction that I hope shortly to see you at Sutton Court, a greater rarity than my travels have afforded me; for believe it, one may go a long way before one meets a friend. Pray write by the post and let me know how you do and what you can tell me of the concernment of your most affectionate friend.'

Locke nevertheless spent much of his life abroad, as he was falsely accused in 1678 of conspiring on behalf of Monmouth, and had to flee the country until the accession of William and Mary.

He never married, but was a great lover of children. John Strachey's half-brother, Samuel Jepp, had left a widow called Elizabeth, with whom Locke claimed cousinship, and her daughter Mary, and later Mary's children were Locke's great favourites. One of his best known works, *Some thoughts concerning Education* was written for Mary's son, Edward Clarke.

After writing to Locke for his advice and finding him encouraging, John Strachey married Jane Hodges, the daughter of a neighbour belonging to a very militant Roundhead family, who survived to become heiress to her father's estates. John died when he was only 40 and she was only 31, and she was left with two small children. Jane refused to marry again, preferring to care for her son and daughter, though eagerly courted by another cousin of Locke's called Lyde. 'My aunt Strachey', wrote Mary's husband Edward Clarke to Locke, 'continues still a widow, notwithstanding the constant solicitations of her importunate lover, your cousin Lyde, who despises all the rest of womankind in comparison with her, and still renews his daily addresses to her with as much confidence as if he had never been rejected.'

John and Jane left just two children, a daughter who married a neighbour, and a son, John, born in 1670, who became a scientist and scholar.

John the younger promised well at Oxford, as Edward Clarke told Locke. 'He is grown tall and very like his father in person and humour, and it is hoped will inherit his learning and virtue also.' His sister, he added, 'has the best education Bristol will afford.'

John grew up, however, to be a very dry, painstaking character, whose main interests were geology, cartography and archaeology. He wrote numerous learned papers and letters to scholarly periodicals, and filled learned notebooks with historical and scientific data. He spent most of his time travelling round the country visiting local societies and investigating records, and was elected a Fellow of the Royal Society in 1719 for 'Achievements in the field of Stratification, particularly as it concerned Coal Mining'. The greater part of his later years he spent in Edinburgh, and he died there in 1743.

He seems also, however, to have exercised some domestic talents, for his first wife bore him no fewer than eighteen children. Not content with this, he married again on her death, and acquired yet one more. Of these a deplorable number died young, most in infancy, though one daughter, Constance, was drowned in a pond in the garden at the age of eleven.

Three sons in the army and one in the navy were all killed without leaving offspring, while one became a doctor and followed in his forebears' footsteps by emigrating to Virginia. There he married a lady called Elizabeth Vernon and had two daughters. When, during the War of Independence, Henry Strachey, the first Baronet and the doctor's nephew, was in America, he made enquiries as to the circumstances of his cousins there, and they replied that they were all in great distress and poverty and appealed for help. This letter is preserved, and there is every reason to suppose that help was sent.

John Strachey, the younger, known in the family as The Antiquarian, had inherited property in London as well as in Somerset, but the burden of his constant travels as well as that of his enormous family, had reduced this very considerably by the time he died. Furthermore his eldest son and heir, Hodges Strachey, was clearly an extravagant nincompoop. Despite three marriages Hodges left no children, but by his death he had managed to dissipate almost all his father had left, starting a series of elaborate and extravagant schemes, all of which came to nothing. When he died, his widow took over the management of the estate, and fared no better than he.

The remaining son of The Antiquarian, Henry, opted out of the family troubles and went to live in Edinburgh, where he married a doctor's daughter of good family, called Helen Clerk. Almost as prolific as his father, he had fifteen children in all, all of whom died except two sons, Henry and John, and two daughters.

Henry was not at all prosperous, but he managed to educate his two sons at Westminster and Oxford and Cambridge, respectively. The elder son, Henry then became a clerk in the War Office, while the younger, John, went into the church.

Their father Henry had not expected to inherit Sutton Court, as there were several brothers older than he, but they were all killed in one war or another before Hodges died. When this occurred Henry left the widow in possession until she too died—in December 1764—leaving Sutton Court mortgaged to the amount of £12,000, with the threat of immediate foreclosure hanging over it. Henry barely had time to realize that Sutton Court was now his responsibility and was about to be lost for ever, for he only lived another six months. He did have time, however, to appeal to his elder son Henry for help, and to learn that help was forthcoming, before he died.

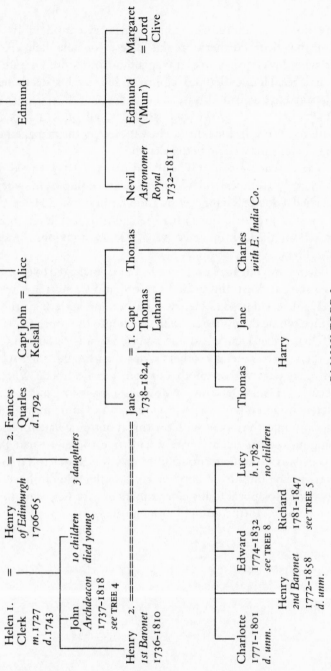

FAMILY TREE 3

IN INDIA WITH CLIVE

Henry Strachey

(1732–74)

Meanwhile history was being made in India by a man who was to have a crucial and unexpected effect on the whole Strachey family future.

At about the same time as the Charter was granted to the Virginia Company, another was granted to the East India Company, optimistically covering not only India, but effectively all Asia. The English were not, however, the only ones in the field. The Dutch and the Portuguese were ahead of them, and the French were soon to follow. Despite their best efforts the English were unable to shift the rich and well-organized Dutch merchant planters from the valuable spice islands, and were forced to fall back on India itself, where the territory was much larger and the Portuguese rather easier to deal with.

When the merchants first arrived and began negotiating for trading rights, it was the comparatively stable India of the great Mogul Emperor, Akbar and his immediate successors, with which they had to deal, but in less than a hundred years the central government in India began to break up, and the resulting violence, uncertainty and corruption made it almost impossible to avoid trouble.

The climate, too, was disastrous. The Company employees went out at about nineteen years old, or earlier, as 'Writers' or clerks. The different ranks on the Civil side, incidentally, continued to be called 'Writers', 'Junior Merchants' and 'Senior Merchants' long after their connection with trade had given place to administration, diplomacy and law. They went to the three main areas where trading had been established, and English 'Factories' built—Madras, Bombay and Calcutta— and had no idea how to live in these unknown and utterly unfamiliar conditions. They wore tight, heavy clothes, and ate and drank far too much; they knew nothing of hygiene and they died like flies. Of 1,200 boys arriving in India in August one year early in the eighteenth century, nearly 500 were dead by the following January. The Company rules were severe, and employees were strictly limited in any trade they wished to conduct on their own account, but they were paid so little that, for those who survived, the temptation to supplement their income surreptitiously and often corruptly, was almost irresistible.

In 1744 a young man called Robert Clive arrived in Madras as a Writer. Like the Stracheys he came of impecunious country gentry, but his character was far more violent and impulsive. He was a man who has been described as headstrong and rapacious, but he was also undoubtedly brilliant.

He soon showed himself to be a first-class military leader in the struggles against the French, and was enthusiastically followed by his Indian troops, who dubbed him Sabit Jung, Steady in War, and when he was 27 he married the sister of his closest friend, Edmund Maskelyne, who had joined her brother in Madras. He now had his first attack of the illness (probably a combination of gallstones and malarial dyspepsia together with a strong manic-depressive tendency) which was to afflict him intermittently throughout his life. He had already, however, contrived to make a good deal of money, with which, among other things, he paid off most of a mortgage on his father's house in Shropshire.

In 1754 he returned to India bringing his wife, Margaret, to whom he was devoted, to Bombay with a young cousin of hers, aged 16, called Jane Kelsall, to keep her company.

Jane—Jenny—was a lively girl, too lively for the staid English colony in Bombay, who disapproved both of her and of Margaret, who was only 19 herself. But Jenny soon married Thomas Latham, Captain of *H.M.S. Tiger*, one of the naval ships on the station. Clive was summoned first to Madras and then to Calcutta, which had been captured by the Nawab of Bengal, charged to recapture the settlement and avenge what was called 'The Outrage of the Black Hole' when 150 English prisoners were incarcerated in one small room overnight, and all but 23 died of heat and thirst.

Clive duly retook Calcutta and defeated the Nawab at the

battle of Plassey. British support was given to a rival Nawab in return for his underwriting a huge punitive fine for the Company, and a large pension, or Jagir, for Clive himself.

After Plassey Clive was anxious to return to England, where he expected to be given a peerage but, willy nilly, he had now become the supreme power in Bengal and he was bogged down, despite his best efforts, in the corruptions and complications of local politics.

When he did finally get home he was given a peerage, but it was an Irish one, less highly regarded than an English one, and he was greatly disappointed. By now, however, he was the equivalent of a multimillionaire, and solaced himself by acquiring country houses—he finally had five spread around the country, as well as a house in London, each larger and grander than the last—and in buying rotten borough seats in the House of Commons for himself and his friends.

In India more and more of the Company's servants hastened to make hay on their own account while they could, and retire as 'Nabobs', until by 1764 the state of affairs in Bengal was so disastrous that Clive was asked to return there and 'clean up the Augean stables'. He agreed on condition that the Company confirmed his Jagir (which they had hitherto refused to do) and gave him full powers.

He envisaged his return with mixed feelings. Oddly enough the Indian climate suited him better than the English one, and power, once tasted, is a heady attraction, but Margaret was pregnant again and could not come with him, and although Jenny Latham was now back in England, a widow with three children, and able to keep Margaret company, Clive and Margaret hated being parted.

This time, however, Clive was determined to take his own staff of supporters with him, including his brother-in-law, 'Mun' Maskelyne as aide, Samuel Ingham, his doctor, and a new man as secretary.

He asked George Grenville, a somewhat pompous but influential friend later to be Prime Minister, to find him an intelligent and reliable man, and Grenville recommended young Henry Strachey of the War Office. Clive and Henry took to each other at once, different as they were, and Clive wrote to Grenville: 'I return you many thanks for Mr Strachey: I have found him in every respect deserving your good opinion.' Later, in the House of Commons he said: 'Many and great are the obligations I have been under [to Mr Grenville], but the greatest of all the obligations was his having recommended to me this gentleman; without his ability and indefatigable industry I could never have gone through my great and arduous undertaking.'

Margaret Clive and Henry Strachey also became great friends. They shared a passion for cats. Margaret had no fewer than two dozen, and Henry sent her a framed tapestry portrait of his own cat, but insisted that it was only a loan, as he valued it greatly himself. Margaret relied heavily on Henry to look after Clive and keep her informed of his state of health when they were apart, and they became frequent correspondents.

Clive and his party set out for India in June 1764, and the journey was a long and tiresome one. The captain was inexperienced; they lost their topmast twice and ran out of stores so that the passengers had nothing to eat for six weeks but pork and pease pudding. They spent two months in Rio and took nearly eleven months in all to reach Calcutta. The worst part of it, according to Clive's letters to Margaret, was Mrs William Sumner, wife of his second-in-command, who played the same two tunes over and over on the harpsichord for four hours a day and insisted on keeping all the doors and windows open so that everyone caught colds.

On their arrival Henry received news of the mortgage on Sutton Court and sought Clive's advice. Clive—no doubt remembering that his own family estate had suffered the same threat—generously insisted on loaning Henry the mortgage money as an advance on his salary, and Sutton Court was saved.

Henry wrote to Lord Willoughby (who was presumably the holder of the mortgage):

Whenever you choose to have the Bond laid off, my father will of course discharge it. Lord Clive has been extremely generous to me and has assured me that the close of our expedition I shall be worth £15,000 which will be entirely out of his pocket, for I have no advantages but a share of those appertaining to his as Governor. The Luxury and Licentiousness of this place is equal to the most incredible accounts in ancient history, but Lord Clive perseveres with a noble disinterestedness and Resolution peculiar to himself to work a Reformation.

Henry did not engage in trade, but he bought some presents and did favours for his friends at home. He asked an agent to procure a diamond for 1,000 rupees (or more if absolutely necessary) to send to his old friend Christopher D'Oyley; he collected medical details about oriental diseases for a London doctor acquaintance, and by the end of his stay reported that Clive had given him £18,000 in all, though Clive himself still made the total under £16,000.

Now back in India Clive started at once on his measures of reform and made some headway. He insisted that all Company servants should sign an undertaking not to receive presents—a step which caused considerable ill-feeling in view of his own Jagir—and put down a mutiny among the officers in Bengal which broke out when he stopped their unofficial perquisites. Henry wrote a cool factual history of this mutiny.

At this point a suggestion arose, mutually agreed by the Mogul Emperor in Delhi, Shah Alam, the Nawab of Bengal, and Clive, that the Company should be entitled to collect the entire revenue of the province for the Emperor. The Emperor in Delhi, the decadent and almost powerless descendant of the great Moguls of the previous centuries, had long been getting none of this revenue, and was delighted at the thought of a fixed percentage, while the Nawab was happy to settle for a peaceful life and an annuity. Clive travelled to Allahabad in the heat of summer—so hot that one of his suite died of it—and there laid on a splendid ceremony for the Granting of the Diwannee (or Revenue). Henry was present, and appears in the huge painting of the event by Benjamin West.

All three parties benefited by this arrangement, for the English turned out to be the most efficient tax-gatherers the province had ever seen. It soon became evident, however, that the grant was a sign that sovereignty and authority, in Bengal at least, had finally passed to the English, however much the Company might try to reject the responsibility.

Clive and his staff returned to England in 1767. Henry only spent two years of his life in India, but it was enough to have a decisive effect on his descendants for a century and a half. While he was there Henry did very valuable work, as Clive freely admitted, for he was a far more competent administrator than his master. He stayed on as secretary, businessman and close friend to Clive and Margaret on their return, and in 1770 he married Margaret's cousin, the widowed Jenny Latham, which made him a member of the family.

On his return Clive, who was again suffering from recurrent bouts of illness, involved himself in fierce quarrels with the Board of the Company, concerning, among other things, the continuance of his famous Jagir.

In 1768, advised by his doctors to go abroad for his health, he took Margaret, Mun, Strachey, Ingham, Jenny and a large train of servants, and set out to tour Europe. They were away for nine months, enjoying social life and generally relaxing. Strachey returned before the others to fight an election to Parliament, strongly supported by Clive.

Henry and Margaret wrote frequently to each other. She called herself his 'Mama' and Clive said that he missed him. They returned at last, with Clive considerably improved in health and able, temporarily at least, to abandon the opium he had been taking for his pain. He was pessimistic about his prospects, however, and wrote to Strachey: 'I fear I must be unhappy as long as I live, though I am certain there is nothing mortal . . . and in all probability I shall drag on a miserable life for fifteen or twenty years longer as I have already done since the year 1752.'

Over the next few years the Company, and with it Clive, became increasingly unpopular. Opposition to the wealth of the Nabobs, of whom Clive was the most prominent, was growing, particularly when the news of the great Bengal famine was received, which was said to have killed nearly a third of the population—even though Clive had no responsibility for that. He had to defend himself in Parliament more than once, and did so with admirable brilliance and spirit. The opposition continued, nevertheless, and at one stage he was made to account fully for all the money he had acquired and spent in India. Among other things he described in detail the moneys he had paid to his own staff, who, he emphasized, were not servants of the Company. In all his expenses came to £85,000 he said, of which £13,049 was paid as salary to Maskelyne, £9,161 to Dr Ingham and £15,942 to Strachey, £12,000 of which was the advance for redeeming Sutton Court.

Eventually a not unfavourable resolution was passed by the House. Clive's winnings were noted, but were not (as he had feared they might be) confiscated, and he was not personally censured.

More and more controversy now arose over the way India should be governed for the Company and by whom. In the end a Governor General was appointed, with authority over all the settlements in India, but a Supreme Council of four advisers was also set up to ensure that the authority should be democratically exercised.

The first Governor General was Warren Hastings, a man of great skill and indubitable intelligence and integrity, whose life was ruined by the baseless persecution of one of his advisers, Philip Francis.

Francis had been a friend and colleague of Henry Strachey's at the War Office, and when he was appointed to the Council he was invited, probably at Henry's suggestion, on a visit to Clive's house Walcot. He was only 33 and on his best behaviour (even losing money at cards without complaint, though he was known to be exceedingly stingy). Clive was not greatly in favour of Hastings, and Francis was happy to take on his opinions and prejudices. He made a good impression on both the Clives, particularly Lady Clive, as he too was a genuine cat lover. She wrote to him soon after his visit in 1773:

Domenico Balestieri [a seventeenth-century Milanese poet] lamented one cat, fallen from the top of a house and crushed to death. I not only one so lost, but two besides, the fathers of families, basely assassinated and put to death by wretched boors, that pretended to believe the lovely creatures were wild and mischievous animals; one fair snowy female hurried out of life by an odious rat at two months old, another overcrammed at Walcot, another still born at Claremont, some of both sexes crushed by doors, others lost by bad nursing, and some hundreds now begging their bread.

On arrival in Calcutta Francis showed himself to be hasty, arrogant and implacably opposed to Warren Hastings. He was admittedly sincere in his view that the Company had no business to stray beyond their commercial activities, but by now such restraint, as Hastings had realized, was pragmatically impossible. Two of the other councillors followed Francis's lead, so that until they succumbed to the Indian climate and died, Hastings was in a perpetual minority and unable to move. Hastings, as is now admitted, was in the right (with some exceptions) but Francis maligned and thwarted him without ceasing for six years, and finally forced a duel on him. In this Francis was wounded, and returned to England, where his prejudiced hostility continued, and caused Hastings to be impeached by Parliament and not cleared for another seven years. Finally, indeed, in 1813, his demeanour and character when called upon to give evidence on Indian matters brought the House to its feet in unprecedented applause and appreciation, but by this time he was 80.

Throughout his spell in India Francis corresponded frequently with Strachey, sought his advice (which was always towards moderation) and endeavoured to persuade him to come out to India and help him (which he declined to do). Henry's letters were, however, full of political news for his friend, and he was ready to undertake errands for him. In January 1775, for instance, soon after Clive's death, he wrote:

At present everything sleeps and everybody too, I believe, except the members of the American Congress, who have petitioned the King for redress of grievances and have fully disavowed the authority of the Legislature. In that case there will infallibly be a change of ministers. . . . Mr Edmund Burke has desired me to recommend to your notice Mr Henry

Hickey, now going to Bengal. If you write me a proper paragraph in answer, I will read it to him, that he may remember you in any compliment in the House of Commons.

Strachey, though he himself does not appear to have been strongly against Hastings, can be blamed for introducing Francis to Clive, and thus enabling him to absorb Clive's prejudices and gain his backing, but Henry's descendants have been active in vindicating Hastings, notably his grandson John, and his great-grandson Lytton, who prepared a Cambridge thesis on the subject in 1905.

Clive, meanwhile, was enduring more and more physical and mental suffering, and Strachey was much concerned to cheer him up and make him take air and exercise. As he wrote to a friend: 'The day being very fine I pressed him to get on horseback. This he assured me was absolutely impossible—that he would never ride more, nay that he would never eat again. I told him that he must, to which he replied very angrily that he would not have his actions controlled but would be his own master. I then left him. In a few minutes he came downstairs, ordered the horses and away we trotted.'

Clive's pessimism soon returned. As he wrote to Henry once again, this time only a few months before his death in 1774, 'How miserable my condition! I have a disease which makes life insupportable, but which doctors tell me won't shorten it an hour. I much fear I must be unhappy as long as I live.'

In November of that year he caught a cold, but decided impetuously to drive from London to Bath in a heavy snow-storm, and ordered his carriage. Henry and Jenny, who was pregnant, were there with the Clives, playing whist while waiting for the carriage to arrive, when Clive, who was feeling ill, retired to the privy and did not return. After some time Henry suggested that Margaret should go and look for him; when she finally found him he had cut his throat with a penknife in an access of despair at his constant pain, and on seeing him lying in his blood, she fainted.

Margaret was a religious woman, and deeply upset at the thought that he had committed the sin of suicide. To spare her feelings it was allowed to be thought (and reported by his early biographers) that he had died of an accidental overdose of opium, but in deference to the belief that suicide was a deadly sin, there is no tablet or monument over his grave in the church of Moreton Saye, near his family home of Styche, in Shropshire.

Margaret finally reconciled herself to the facts and lived on for over forty years. Jenny, many years later, gave an eyewitness account of the event to her son, the younger Henry, who took notes and passed the story on to his nephew Edward. Edward published a full account in the 1880s, so that the truth about the suicide finally became known.

In his Will Clive left Henry £400 and made him Executor and Guardian of his son Edward, the second Lord Clive, who also remained a lifelong friend of the Strachey family.

The elder Clive's public personality was never an engaging one, but he clearly had the power to make and keep good personal friends, as not only were his family extremely fond of him, but his close associates, Strachey among them, defended him strongly and remained loyal for life.

4

THE AMERICAN WAR

Sir Henry Strachey

(1774–1810)

Clive had obtained a seat in Parliament for Henry in December 1768, while he and his party were touring Europe, and Henry remained a member almost continuously until he retired in 1807 at the age of 71. He served for a number of constituencies, Pontefract in Yorkshire, Bishop's Castle near one of Clive's homes on the Welsh border, Saltash near Plymouth and East Grinstead in Sussex. He also held several minor ministerial posts, among others Under Secretary at the Treasury and later at the Home Office, as well as serving on advisory and drafting committees in the House.

He found Sutton Court too distant from his political work, and rarely went there, but lived in Park Street, in London, where all his five children were born.

He and Jenny were a remarkably loving couple, suited to each other in every way and devoted to their children, and the last thing Henry ever wanted was to be separated from her. In 1776, however, the rebellion of the American Colonies, about which he had written to Philip Francis the previous year, had reached a crucial stage from a diplomatic as well as a military point of view—as well, incidentally, as nearly ruining the East India Company, which depended to a great extent on its exports of tea to America.

The British party system of Government was at that time in a very confused state. The young King George III was determined to take a hand in Government himself, and to insist on what he regarded as his right and duty to choose ministers who would follow his policies, but circumstances forced him to temporize.

He could not tolerate the idea of yielding to colonial pressure, and did not believe it could prevail. The country, insofar as it knew what was going on, and the politicians, were however much more mixed in their reactions. There was considerable sympathy for the colonists, whose stand, after all, only echoed that of Parliament itself 150 years earlier. But by the same token the one unshakeable absolute upon which the English would not yield was the authority of Parliament in which, of course, the Colonists were not represented.

Subject to this proviso, the more open-minded members of both parties, including Chatham, Pitt, Fox, Burke, Lord Shelburne and even the Prime Minister, Lord North, were to a greater or lesser extent in favour of conciliation, but nevertheless a greater number demanded purely punitive force.

Among those who sought peace was a nobleman called Lord Howe, a competent Admiral, and a kindly if not scintillating man. Lord Howe believed that he, and he alone, had the answer to the question of peace with the colonists, and would be able to negotiate successfully with George Washington. He was thought to be the illegitimate grandson of George I, and whatever the truth of this, he was regarded with approval by the King, and succeeded in being appointed Commander-in-Chief of the North American Naval Station and also head of a Commission set up to negotiate peace with the rebels.

Howe was determined to use his own methods in this matter, and to modify without consultation the unyielding brief he carried from the King and Government. He believed that some successful accommodation could be achieved if the British would only refrain from hardening the opposition by adopting extreme arguments. What he and other well-intentioned politicians did not realize was that time, distance and shortsighted financial oppression had already pushed the colonists too far for conciliation of any kind to be acceptable.

Henry Strachey, as an experienced negotiator and drafter, was asked to go with Howe as Secretary to the Commission. He was not at all anxious to undertake so distant and unpromising a mission, or to leave Jenny for what might be a long time, but when Lord North, the Prime Minister, came over to sit beside him in Parliament and urged him to accept, he finally agreed, on condition that he was paid not only £5 a day but a pension of £400 a year when the affair was over.

Henry was far from being a mercenary man, but he knew what it was to be poor; he was dependent on what he earned, and, unlike Clive, had brought no fortune back with him from India. He wrote frankly about money to Christopher D'Oyley, Under Secretary at the Colonial Office, who was a close friend of both the Stracheys and had recommended Henry for the post.

Henry complained to him that the Commission's payments were 'docked for monstrous vails to the Treasury and the Exchequer. That diminution,' he went on, 'is abominably shabby towards the Commissioners, who must maintain some degree of state in a country where at least the luxuries of life are very expensive. These bagatelles would have been no object to me if my hands had not been as clean as you, and perhaps only you, know they were in the land of gold and silver.'

He sailed with Lord Howe in H.M.S. Eagle in June 1776, modestly assuring his wife: 'My mind is perfectly at ease with respect to the weight of Business I have undertaken. I shall go through it with Diligence and Fidelity, which will stand me instead of Ability, and pass, as they have done before, for a tolerable substitute.'

To his friend Governor Tonyn in Florida he wrote: 'Above all things the very handsome manner in which the Proposition was made to me (wherein I confess, my interest as well as my vanity were concerned) prevailed upon me to embark with Lord Howe in this business.'

Henry knew and liked Lord Howe, but was himself of a far more realistic cast of mind, and though he disapproved strongly of the rebels, he doubted if the Commission's task was a possible one.

Lord Howe's brother, General Howe, took over command of the army at Boston. Whether he was pursuing the same tactics as his brother or whether he was merely lazy and incompetent, as his critics maintained, the fact remains that though he succeeded in winning a number of individual battles in the forthcoming campaign, on no occasion did he push on to destroy the opposing army, and the English at home became more and more impatient and scornful.

Meanwhile Lord Howe finally arrived off Sandy Hook, after what Henry called 'a boisterous journey with stands of ice and thick fog'. Barely a week earlier, on 4th July, the Declaration of Independence had been signed, and to Henry at least this meant that a final break was inevitable. Indeed he believed that the signing had been rushed forward to face Howe with a *fait accompli*.

General Howe nonetheless pushed on and succeeded in taking New York by August, while his brother, anxious to temper victory with sweet reason, summoned a Conference with the Americans on Long Island, to which, somewhat reluctantly, Benjamin Franklin, John Adams and Samuel Routledge agreed to come.

Howe explained his hopes, and introduced Henry, who was taking the Minutes, to the Americans, but they were not impressed either by Howe or by his policy. The French Ambassador, commenting on the event, said that 'Henry Strachey was a man of merit', but Lord Howe was 'very muddled'.

The Commission settled down to winter in New York. Lord Howe was hopeful that the war was nearly over, but Henry was sure it would last another year or more, and in fact it lasted more than five. He loathed the climate, was unwell and homesick and his one solace was his correspondence with Jenny.

As the winter wore on, they wrote to each other by every possible ship. Henry was now 40; they had been married for six years, and already had three children, and their letters show the trusting and teasing affection they had for each other.

Soon after the Commission arrived, Jenny had written to Henry to ask him for a lock of his hair, and he had answered:

I recollect this moment that in one of your letters you desire a lock of my hair—I will send it by the next opportunity, unless I should find that you are more likely soon to have my whole head. Would that I could repose it I know where this very night. When that pleasing idea rises (which it foolishly does too often) it banishes every other and proves that my heart is unalterably yours. The finishing of a letter to you always resembles a real Parting, the Pain of which I hope never to suffer again.

By the time they reached New York he was more cheerful and the lock was finally sent. It was not yet grey, he assured her, and he added: 'I expect you to return me a lock of yours, which I propose to carry always about me as an Amulet to preserve me against the influence of American charms. You may also send me some of the Children's hair. But I charge you not to tell anybody that the Secretary to the Commission is such a silly fellow as to write even to his wife upon these trifles.'

Jenny wrote back: 'I every moment entertain a secret hope that the next half hour may bring me some news of my beloved.' and sent him her love by a Captain Bellew. Henry teased her in return. 'He said he had a thousand messages, kisses and I know not what for me—I desired him to call upon me and deliver all but the kisses—those I allowed him to keep. If you would send me a few by a woman I should have no objection. I think I should like them if the bearer were handsome.'

'In justice to myself,' replied Jenny, 'I must assure you that jealousy is not in the catalogue of my faults, nor has this vile passion, I thank God, ever interrupted my peace for one moment of my life.'

She fussed about his health, and told him how much she missed him, and about the children, and how they had already grown since he had left. Of their second son Edward, then only three, she said: 'You are acquainted my dear Harry, with all your children but little Edward, who has ripened into understanding since his dear Father's departure. He has none of the "mauvais honte" which is common to children a little older than himself. He speaks as plain as his brother and sister, and with a pair of intelligent black eyes attracts everybody's notice. He attacks strangers in the Park, and asks them questions; if they are well disposed he calls them "Gentleman", if otherwise it is only "Man".'

She also sent him news of his stepson, Bob Latham, son of her first marriage, who was joining the East India Company as a Civilian.

Jenny tried to keep in touch with Henry's brother John, who was now an Archdeacon, but found his manners depressing. 'He civilly asked after every individual member of my family,' she wrote after one of his visits, 'but that affectionate kind cordiality which I should wish always to subsist between me and your brother was wanting. These interviews always sink my spirits, for he is capable of being agreeable and I have such a desire to be well with him that I am always hurt when I find it cannot be.'

Henry's reply showed little brotherly sympathy. 'I am sorry your attention to the Doctor is so ill received. But why subject yourself to his humours? If he does not behave with that civility which is your due, I don't see why you should be afraid of telling him so.' Jenny was less brusque and noted: 'The Doctor has not said anything to vex me for a long time, and I forgive him all that is past.'

In the summer of 1777 Lord Cornwallis headed the British forces in the south and was making his way north, while Burgoyne was pushing south from Canada to support General Howe. Despite several unsuccessful engagements, the British finally managed to take the capital, Philadelphia, and the Army and the Commission both spent the winter there.

The political situation was more or less stagnant, but life was much pleasanter in Philadelphia than in New York. Henry wrote to Jenny in early spring: 'You know that during the whole of last winter I never was at one play, Concert or Assembly, nor visited any one of the Ladies. This did not proceed from a natural indifference to the fair sex in particular but from a miserable state of health which rendered me unfit for the enjoyment of either. During our long voyage hither, I mended, but even upon our arrival at this place I was very far from well.'

Things were better now, however. 'I ride 2 or 3 hours every day,' he continued, 'and sometimes dance into the bargain, for though I don't wear a red coat I'd have you know that I make my Party good amongst the Philadelphia ladies. As I get on in health I visibly grow fat. My upper leg is already almost as stout as yours—and that's a bold word!'

There were worries which he did not pass on to Jenny. Not long before his arrival in America Henry had somewhat rashly invested in a small indigo plantation in East Florida, with 30 slaves. He could not, of course, supervise this himself, and the agent he employed turned out to be a rogue and a drunkard. He tried to get his friend Tonyn, who was Governor of Florida, to keep an eye on the property, but the war caught up with them and he lost more and more money. In all he had invested more than £5,000 of his meagre capital, and now tried to salvage what he could by switching from indigo to lumber, which could be sold in the West Indies, and was not subject to the risks of an ocean crossing. He still had little success and after the war, when the territory was ceded to Spain, he was forced to cut his losses and squeeze what he could out of compensation.

Meanwhile less and less progress was being made by the Commission in face of the complete refusal of the Americans to compromise. Henry had had little to do during the two years that the Commission had been in operation but to draft letters to Washington which—since Lord Howe insisted on addressing them to plain 'Mr' Washington, denying his title of General— brought few replies and no satisfaction, and to set up a cypher correspondence with General Charles Lee, an American traitor who was secretly in touch with the British, and who was finally court-martialled by Washington in 1778.

In October 1777 the British under Burgoyne suffered a shameful defeat at Saratoga. When the news reached home, the Howes—General Howe in particular—became more unpopular than ever, and early in 1778 the General was recalled and forced to resign. It was becoming clear even to the optimistic Lord Howe that he was getting nowhere, and he too finally applied to come home. While he was setting his affairs in order with the Fleet, in Rhode Island, Henry stayed in Philadelphia, quartered with some of the General's staff, and he wrote to Jenny describing the kind of life they were managing to lead.

At nine o'clock a Regiment parades under our window and salutes us with a piece or two of execrable music. After breakfast we follow our own Inventions. I amuse myself amongst my books, if I have no writing business, unless the weather and my Humour incline me to walk out and vary the scene by dropping into agreeable families, of which there are a few. . . . I have strove to avoid dining out but have at last fallen a little into it. Here's a card on my Chimney piece from General Pattison, and having excused myself some time ago, I must dine with him next Tuesday. He is a Jemmy Gentleman—quite the Pink of Curtesy and Politeness.

There are large Tea drinkings (the most fashionable Party) where one may go, and I sometimes do to talk nonsense. The Young Lady who makes and dispenses that favourite Liquor thinks herself a very eminent personage. The table is decorated with many more cups than are necessary and a Silver Kitchen completes the ornamental part of the Repast. But this is nothing unless the presiding Goddess has at least one Beau next her, who pays his whole adoration to her alone. If he wishes to be thought gallant he must stick to her and be in hot water during the ceremony, which is never of short duration.

Every Monday we have a play; they are usually well performed. The Play House is as large as that at Brussels. Sir William has one of the boxes; I am always of his Party and it is an entertainment I never miss.

Every Thursday we have a Ball at the Rooms. There are generally about 30 ladies, all Dancers, and they don't come with what you call Chaperones. . . . Six ladies dined with [Sir William] last Tuesday. Two recruits came in the evening and these eight jugged it away till 2 in the morning. You won't suppose me a sick man when I add that I did not sit down the whole evening. Notwithstanding this debauch I was up yesterday by 7. Though I have given you rather a gay sketch of my life and conversation, you must not imagine that I am a perfect Idler. I sometimes do business—and I always wish that the Times would alter so as to demand every hour for business.

It was May 1778 before General Howe sailed, and September before Lord Howe, too, could return. When he got back he was forced to defend himself in Parliament, and while the charges which had been brought against him were withdrawn, he was deeply humiliated. He resigned both from the Commission and from his naval post, citing his health and the treatment his brother had received, and a new set of Commissioners was appointed.

Henry was extremely anxious to return home too, but he was concerned about the possibility of losing his pension. As he wrote to Jenny in March 1778:

> I still wish to have a hand in the great Work of Peace even at the expense of a little longer absence. You must however always understand that if any Changes of Commissioners should take place, no Consideration whatsoever shall induce me to hold the Secretaryship. Our friend Mr D'Oyley will, I trust, upon such an event take care that I be *superseded* for I fear that my title to the pension would be disputed upon my voluntary resignation. The words of the Patent are clear enough, viz "On my being dispossessed of the Office or the Expiration of the Com-mission." which last Condition might admit of a Quibble.

A month later he was still worried.

> I cannot help being extremely anxious. I hope and trust D'Oyley has taken care that another Secretary shall be appointed in the new Commission. I cannot, will not, stay after Lord Howe obtains his release. I came to serve with him, not with strangers, nor would I serve with them (whoever they may be, for we have not yet learnt their names) for any consideration, even if the climate and every other important circumstance of life rendered my stay abroad a matter of indifference. Indeed I can hardly think they will expect it, for if they appoint a parcel of new commissioners I have a good Right to *say* I ought to have been one, and to *affect* to be angry at being so slighted. I fervently hope that my name is *not* included in any capacity or that my continuance is, at least, left entirely to my own option.

He got his pension—£547 per annum for life—and by the end of 1778 was home with Jenny, and for a while life was calm again. During the time he was in America he had been able to do some favours for a Colonel Clerk, who was probably a cousin of his mother, Helen Clerk, and in return Colonel Clerk left him a house called Rook's Nest. This was in Surrey, not far from Clive's mansion, Claremont, and within easy reach of town, and all the

Stracheys were very fond of the place and spent much of their time there. Two of Henry's aunts lived at Sutton Court, but Henry seldom visited the place. His brother-in-law, Tom Kelsall, who suffered from rheumatism and took the waters at Bath occasionally, looked after his interests there.

Two more children were born after Henry returned, Richard in 1781 and Lucy in 1782. His elder daughter, Charlotte, died unmarried at 30, while Lucy married a man only noted, a later Strachey reported, for 'fox-hunting and port wine drinking'. She had no children.

In 1780 Jenny's son, Bob Latham, now with the Indian Civil Service in Madras, volunteered to fight in the Second Mysore War against Hyder Ali. He was one of the few survivors after the destruction of Colonel Baillie's detachment at Polilur in that war, and with several others he was imprisoned in chains for three and a half years. The prisoners finally contrived to get news of their whereabouts carried out, written very small, in the stem of a quill, and their release was obtained. The message itself is still among the Strachey papers. It is about 8 by 2 inches, and carries 29 lines of minute writing, most of which is an apology to his mother for his want of love and duty in the past.

In America the fighting continued. The British in the south, under Lord Cornwallis, were protected by their ships which prevented the enemy from bringing in military supplies. Help, however, was now beginning to reach the Americans from Europe.

Ever since 1763, when they had lost the Seven Years' War and with it the province of Canada, the French had been looking for a chance of revenge against Britain. In 1778, after receiving the news of Saratoga, they seized the opportunity of forming an alliance against the hated enemy and signed a treaty with the new American nation. Benjamin Franklin, who had gone to France as an unofficial representative in 1776, was now accepted as official Ambassador, and prevailed upon the French to send vital military supplies for Washington in their ships. Spain, like France, was violently opposed to Britain, and was much concerned to safe-guard, and if possible extend, its American and West Indian possessions. Though disinclined to ally itself with a rebellious democracy, it too finally joined France in 1779 in declaring war on Britain. Other nations took heart from the British misfortunes—as they say, all the other tigers are charmed when one tiger loses its tail—and joined a 'neutral' alliance.

In 1781 the French navy was at last able to take effective action to isolate the British forces in the Southern states, and in October Cornwallis was forced to surrender to Washington and the war was over.

News of the disaster reached England early in 1782, and Lord North resigned. Rockingham was leader of the Opposition party, but his right-hand man was Fox, whom the King loathed, so he ordered Rockingham to form a coalition with the less extreme Shelburne with instructions to avoid war in Europe and bring about a satisfactory peace in America—no easy task.

Henry was offered a post as Under Secretary in the Treasury in this Government, and though by conviction he was a mid-stream Tory, he was happy in the circumstances to accept it.

Four months later, however, Rockingham died, Shelburne took over, and all appointments were in the melting pot. One day Henry met Fox—who had no liking for Shelburne—on Hay Hill, and Fox asked him: 'What will they do with you?' Strachey replied: 'Lord Shelburne says I shall keep my place,' and Fox retorted: 'Then by God, you're out!'

He was indeed out of that post, but was found another, even if it was not so advantageous from the financial point of view. On 25th July 1782, he wrote to John Walsh, who was a relative of Jenny's and a co-executor with Henry of Clive's Will. 'I have not hitherto had time to give you an account of my fate,' he wrote.

> Lord Shelburne, after keeping me twelve days in suspense, sent for me only to communicate his intention of putting Mr Orde (latterly his Under Secretary of State) in my room, and Mr Rose in the room of Dick Burke. He gave me by way of Compensation, a profusion of fine speeches, offered me the Board of Admiralty (which by the way he had filled up two days before) and said there was nothing I could ask he would not grant. Not being disposed to receive any Obligation from him, I took my leave. In about half an hour after this

Conference, I was invited in the handsomest manner by Mr
Townshend to be Under Secretary of State in his Department.
I asked him but one question, which was, whether Lord
Shelburne had anything to do with the offer he made me—and
upon his assuring me that he had not, and that it was by no
means his own meaning to make a Party man of me, I accepted.
The Office is called the Home Department, in which is included India and America. Mr Townshend is a pleasant open
man, and I am hitherto perfectly satisfied with my situation
except in point of emolument. The Treasury would have
produced me about four thousand a year honestly; and my
present employment is scarcely worth eight hundred. We have
however borne our downfall with great philosophy and are all
in good health.

As soon as Lord North fell, it was decided to open peace talks
with the Americans, and in April 1782 these began unofficially
in Paris. At that time Benjamin Franklin, now accepted as
Ambassador to France, was the only authorized American in
Paris, while the man sent from London was a prominent Scottish
merchant, known to Shelburne for over twenty years, who had
large estates in America and the West Indies and was already
friendly with Franklin.

The French government insisted on being involved in the
terms of any agreement, and Franklin was joined by John Jay,
who had been the Envoy in Spain, and later by John Adams from
the Netherlands. The proceedings, however, were less than
professional; with the exception of Franklin himself none of the
negotiators were experienced in the art; they were all, as Adams
admitted, 'Militia Diplomatists'. The Americans were not on
good terms with each other or with the French Foreign Minister,
Vergennes, who was not anxious for the Americans to win too
great a success, and they were too far away to consult with their
own government.

The negotiations became official in September and started on a
high note. The French put in 'arrogant and lofty' claims for
Canada, the Nova Scotia–Newfoundland fisheries and Grenada,
in addition to other concessions including some in India, where-

Above left: John Strachey (1634-74); *right:* The Widow Baber (artist unknown). Elizabeth Cross, who married William Strachey in 1634, and later Edward Baber. Known in the family as 'Born Cross'.
Below: 'The Twenty Children'. Some of the 19 children of John Strachey the Antiquarian (1671-1743), showing Sutton Court in the background. Artist unknown

Left: Lord Clive by Nathaniel Dance. One of several very similar paintings by Dance, this one given by Clive to Sir Henry Strachey

Below left: Sir Henry's tapestry cat

Below: Henry Strachey, 1st Baronet (1736–1810) by James Northcote

Above: The Granting of the Diwanee, by Benjamin West. (Sir Henry Strachey is in front of the left-hand pillar, with his head turned to the left). *Below:* The American Commissioners, by Benjamin West *Left to right:* John Jay (standing), John Adams (seated), Benjamin Franklin and William Temple Franklin (seated), Henry Laurens (behind). The last two did not sign the final treaty

Archdeacon Strachey (1737–1816) and his family, by Sir William Beechey

Richard Strachey (1781–1847)
in middle age, by William Patten

Sir Henry Strachey, 2nd Baronet
(1772–1858), by William Patten

upon the British warned the Americans not to tie themselves too closely to their allies in pushing terms which would have to be rejected, whatever the cost.

The Americans then put in their own claims, and the British negotiator, Oswald, was, in the opinion of his government, far too yielding. He admitted to Franklin that Britain had been 'foolishly involved in four wars' and that peace was 'absolutely necessary'. Franklin hopefully suggested that Britain should freely cede Canada and the fisheries to America, and, according to his report of the conversation Oswald liked the idea, and 'we parted exceedingly good friends'.

Oswald shuttled back and forth and was instructed by Shelburne to be firmer. Meanwhile Fox, the Foreign Secretary, anxious to rival Shelburne, sent his own negotiator, George Grenville, son of the man who had recommended Strachey to Clive, reporting only to himself, to deal with Vergennes, so that everyone worked at cross-purposes and confusion reigned.

Finally Townshend complained that Oswald was 'credulous and weak', and wrote to the Prime Minister: 'I would not want to have anything said from me to Mr Oswald, but I think it necessary that he should know that he has been in my opinion a great deal too easy . . . so as to appear to all here to have been quite in the hands of Mr Franklin and Mr Jay.'

Shelburne agreed and wrote to Oswald: 'I am open to every good impression you give us of Mr Jay, but I find it difficult if not impossible to enter into the policy of all that you recommend upon the subject both of the fishery and the boundaries, and of the principle which you seem to have adopted of going before the Commissioners in every point of favour or confidence. . . . Such a maxim is not only new in all negotiations, but I consider it as no way adapted to our present circumstances, but as diametrically opposed to our interests in the present moment.'

Negotiations were at too delicate a stage for Oswald to be sacked, but Townshend suggested that his Under Secretary, Henry Strachey, should be sent over to 'stiffen' him and insist on points the Cabinet wanted agreed. Shelburne thought this was a good idea and it was done, and before Henry left, Shelburne gave him a detailed verbal briefing. He was to do his best to retain the

'Back Lands' (Western Canada, Maine and Nova Scotia) for the dispossessed Loyalists, though even more important was the question of financial compensation, so near to the hearts of the British oligarchy. Henry was not empowered to sign, but was to have a virtual veto over Oswald and to share the considerable responsibility with him.

He arrived in Paris on 28th October and Oswald magnanimously welcomed him and found quarters for him in his own hotel, considering their undertaking too important to indulge in hurt feelings.

Henry now began in real earnest to have a hand in 'the great work of Peace' and horse-trading and argument proceeded at all hours of the day and night. Henry wrote to Townshend: 'Several of the Expressions, being too loose, should be tightened, for the Americans are the greatest Quibblers I ever knew.' The Americans found him a much tougher proposition than Oswald, and John Adams, who had arrived in Paris two days before Henry, reported to Congress: 'Strachey is as artful and insinuating a man as they could send; he pushes and presses every point as far as it can possibly go. He has a most eager, earnest, pointed spirit.'

Britain's position was not strong, and at one point Henry had to return to London for fresh instructions, enduring a rough crossing on the way. He won some important concessions on the territorial front—the retention of Canada and the Nova Scotia–Newfoundland fisheries, for instance, insisting that the Americans should be granted the 'liberty' and not the 'right' to use these, but the question of the Loyalists was much harder to solve, despite Henry's ingenious suggestion that particularly obnoxious Loyalists might be excluded from the benefits. As Franklin told him: 'Your Ministers require that we should receive again into our bosoms those who have been our enemies and restore their properties who have destroyed ours; and this while the wounds they have given us are still bleeding.'

In the end the best Henry could achieve on this point was a compromise wording stating that a full restoration of the rights and properties of the Loyalists was to be 'earnestly recommended' by Congress to the legislatures of the various States.

Congress, being too far off, had not even been consulted over this, and were not pleased, but in fact it bound them to nothing and was merely something of a face-saver for the British, and a sop for the raging anti-Americanism that had now developed in Parliament and the country.

Although the Americans had undertaken to consult the French government before signing the Treaty, they were anxious to avoid the delays and discussions involved in including a third party, and despite Franklin's protests they did not inform Vergennes in advance. The French were furious, and Franco-American relations suffered a severe set-back, which delighted the British Cabinet.

Henry posted back to London, leaving Oswald to sign the preliminary Peace Treaty at the end of November, and to pay generous tribute to Henry for his part in it. Nothing, as he wrote to Townshend, could have exceeded 'the indefatigable persever-ance with which he disputed inch by inch those points of the ground which we were finally forced to recede from'.

Henry was exhausted, and just before leaving he wrote to Nepean, a friend and colleague in the Home Office; 'Now are we to be hanged or applauded, for thus rescuing you from the American War. . . . I am half dead with perpetual anxiety and shall not be at ease until I see how the Great Men receive me. If this is not as good a Peace as was expected, I am confident it is the best that could have been made. . . . I shall set off tomorrow, hoping to arrive on Wednesday, if I am alive. God forbid I should ever have a hand in another Peace!'

The Great Men were not happy about the outcome, but it was Shelburne who suffered the most; he fell to Fox and North, and never again held office. But Britain had, after all, been defeated, a fate which had not befallen her for a long while, and could not expect to achieve all she had hoped for. On the other hand, Shelburne's main objective had been a peace which would renew good relations and trade with the Americans, and separate them from their dangerous allies, and both aims had been achieved.

Two years later Henry made his peace with Shelburne in a handsome manner. On 15th September 1785 he wrote to him:

I will freely own, My Lord, that there was a time when I had the mortification of suspecting that I was not in possession of your good opinion. But whatever were my reflections upon that occasion I can say with the greatest truth that your Lordship's subsequent conduct was so manly, so distinct and so unreserved, as to give me a consequence in my own eyes not inferior to that which I must have obtained in the Office of which you had so lately deprived me. . . . My veneration for your character was at the same time confirmed by my observation of your public conduct, which fell officially under my view. The making of a Peace is always hazardous to the popularity of a Minister. But the measure was absolutely necessary to the salvation of your country, and you nobly dared to cut the Gordian Knot. . . . For myself I was never a Party Man. But from habit I am fond of Business and in the various situations into which almost mere Chance has thrown me, my own credit and the Honor of my Employers have always been my only objects. Having religiously maintained those principles in the early part of my life when a Deviation from them might have been convenient to my private fortune, I shall probably retain them in any future Office which I may happen to find in the Wheel of Politics. . . . Your regard, My Lord, cannot but be considered as a very distinguished Honor, and although it should never be in your power to give me any public mark of your Attention, I shall ever feel and acknowledge that I am, in truth, my Lord, your Lordship's most obliged and faithful servant.

In spite of the flowery language and obsequious formalities, he was obviously sincere.

The Americans ordered a portrait of the negotiating Commissioners of the Treaty of Paris to be painted by the American artist, Benjamin West. It shows the four Americans, the heavy figure of Benjamin Franklin with his colleagues on the left of the table, but on the right, where we should expect to find the British team, there is plain unpainted canvas. On meeting West, many years later, John Adams' son, John Quincy Adams, strongly regretted this, and urged the painter to complete the picture. West, however, claimed that he had no likeness of Oswald to work from, owing to the fact that the man was one-eyed and conscious of having an unprepossessing appearance, and had therefore always avoided being painted. Henry was not an actual signatory of the Treaty, though he took a major part in the negotiations and had been given joint responsibility with Oswald, and it is interesting to note that West had in fact already painted a likeness of him in Clive's big picture of the Granting of the Diwannee. A likeness of Caleb Whitefoord, secretary to the Commission, also exists, and it seems a pity that West did not pursue the matter.

Henry led a peaceful life after this. He was made Keeper of Stores, Ordnance and Ammunition the following year, and Master of the King's Household from 1794 to 1805. Henry took a particular interest in the royal gardens and George III clearly had a good opinion of him, as on 30th May 1801 he wrote to one of the gardeners, a Mr Eaton:

> The King during his stay at Kew, has frequently examined the Kitchen Garden, and very much approves of Mr Eaton's Manner of conducting it; besides being much pleased with his candid manner of confessing that all Mr Strachey's Regulations as to the manner of settling the contracts are perfectly just. His Majesty is desirous to put all the Gardens under the direction of Mr Strachey; he therefore would have an Estimate made for keeping the Queen's Garden in town, and if Mr Robinson declines holding it on these terms, that Mr Eaton may be appointed for that purpose; the Saving will I trust enable Mr Strachey to take on him the Expence of the Botanical Garden at Kew.

While in this post Henry appointed his daughter Lucy as 'housemaid or ladies maid or deputy cinder-woman' as his grandson Edward described the position, from which she drew a salary for a number of years. He also made the old gardener at Sutton Court, John Burrow, Rat-catcher to the King.

In 1801 he was given a Baronetcy, and chose a motto to accompany his arms. This was 'Coelum non Animum', a quotation from Horace, 'Coelum non animum mutant'—They change their skies but not their minds.

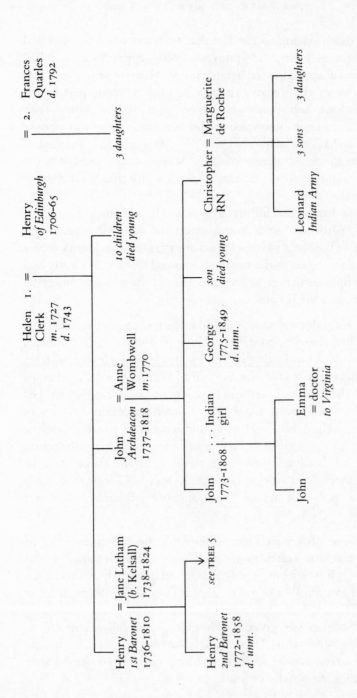

FAMILY TREE 4

5

The Archdeacon's Family and the Second Sir Henry

(1737–1818)

Henry's younger brother, John, born in Edinburgh in 1737, was an anomaly in the Strachey family, a man who made a career as an Anglican clergyman. He went to Westminster school at the same time as Henry, and was awarded a scholarship to Trinity College, Cambridge, taking his M.A. in 1763 and receiving an LL.D. in 1770. There is no reason to suppose that he was not a religious man, but it is not impossible that he shared, to some extent at least, the family scepticism, since at that time the Church was perhaps more often a career than a vocation.

We do know that he was a difficult man. When his sister-in-law, Jenny Strachey, complained to her husband that his brother had been cold and ill-mannered to her, and had not answered her letters, Henry wrote back: 'He is very touchy. His temper is such that he generally exerts his ingenuity to discover reasons to condemn rather than to excuse, which I should think must torment himself as well as others. However he is my brother and therefore I know you would not wilfully quarrel with him.'

John was fond of money, and managed to assemble a good amount in the course of his life. He was also undoubtedly learned. He was elected a Fellow of the London Society of Antiquarians and was responsible for the publication of six folio volumes of the Rolls of Parliament from the time of Edward I to Henry VII.

He married Anne Wombwell, daughter of a prominent London merchant, who almost certainly brought him a handsome dowry, and he lived until 1818, becoming in turn Rector, Prebendary and Archdeacon, spending some time in Vienna, which he hated, thereafter as Chaplain to the Bishop of Norwich, and finally Chaplain in Ordinary to King George III.

When John returned from Vienna, after their father's death, Henry was in India with Clive. John wrote to Henry:

28 April 1766: Dear Harry. . . . My having been obliged to leave Vienna on account of my health and my connections with the Bishop of Norwich will be no news to you. I find him and his Lady extremely agreeable and think my Servitude will be very tolerable. We set off for our Diocese in about a fortnight. In the meantime I fancy Mr D'Oyley means to send me again down to Sutton etc whither I have already been to shew the tenants that the Family is not quite extinct, and to prevent unwarrantable Liberties being taken with the Estates, which is generally the case when the Heir is abroad, and when none of his Relations appear from time to time on the premises. I have ever since my return to England had daily proofs how much your penetration surpassed mine with regard to——* I congratulate you that my Father's Will does not oblige you to have much dealing with Her. Should I not be alive at your return Messrs D'Oyley and Rose can conjointly furnish you with anecdotes; but your own understanding will enable you to see this through a Veil which she may find expedient to put on again, for her interest. . . . It is with pleasure that I am able to acquaint you that young Mr Jones (who was supposed to stand in our Way) died about a month since, on his travels. I cannot wish the Ladies' death;† they do a great deal of good and they would be a great Loss to the Neighbourhood. I have told D'Oyley of this Windfall; it is a *distant* project as they are both in very good health. I think no notice whatever should be taken of it in your letters to England, for fear our Expectations should come round to the Ladies' ears and thereby be frustrated.

While he was Chaplain to the King, family tradition has it that on one occasion the monarch, whose eyesight was then very poor and his wits fading, nevertheless recognized the Archdeacon. 'I knew it was little Strachey by the voice,' he said. No doubt this

---

* Presumably their stepmother, Frances Strachey.

† The Ladies were probably Henry's aunts, who lived at Sutton Court but were on such bad terms that they had their apartments walled off from each other, and used different staircases.

was the same voice that was later to become celebrated in Bloomsbury as the 'Strachey voice'.

Although a small man, he was the handsome father of ten handsome children, four sons and six daughters. Nothing much is known of the daughters, except that one apparently lived to be 99 without marrying.

The eldest son, John, following his cousins, Sir Henry's sons, became a Writer in the East India Company service, acting, as most of the family did, as Persian translator and magistrate (Persian being the language spoken by the ruling classes in India at that time). He never married, but had two children by an Indian mother, John and Emma. They were educated in England, and Emma married a doctor and went to live in Virginia— following another family tradition.

The third son died young, and the youngest, Christopher, served with distinction in the Navy in the Napoleonic Wars. His career seems in many respects to have been a pattern for the Hornblower novels of C. S. Forester; he took part in the battle of 'The Glorious First of June' in 1794, became a Captain and was captured by the French in 1807, after a gallant but unsuccessful attempt to run his ship, *HMS Dauntless*, up the Vistula. Napoleon himself, according to family records, praised him for this, saying that the feat '*mérite d'être mise sur la page de l'histoire*'. He was decorated as Knight of the Imperial Order of St Vladimir by the Russians, spent seven years as a prisoner of the French, and there converted to Catholicism (which must have distressed his father) and married Marguerite de Roche, daughter of Chevalier de Roche, a Lieutenant Colonel of Infantry, though they later separated. He had four sons, (one of whom, Leonard joined the Army in India and was the only one to have any children) and three daughters, the sons being brought up as Protestants and the daughters as Catholics.

George Strachey, the second son, born in 1775, went to Westminster school and there made friends with Robert Southey, later to become poet Laureate and biographer of Nelson.

Southey, on his arrival, as was the school custom, was placed in the care of the somewhat older Strachey, as 'Shadow' to his 'Substance'. Now close friends, they planned with two others,

Grosvenor Bedford and William Wynn, an impertinent school paper to be called *The Flagellant*. This was not a happy undertaking for Southey, as it not only resulted in his being expelled from the school but was also, in all probability, the main cause of a serious quarrel between him and George, though we do not know the details. In 1792 George wrote to Southey saying that 'perhaps the Flagellant was the cause' and claiming that Southey was entirely to blame.

The breach was indeed far more bitter on the Strachey side than on the side of Southey, who, despite repeated efforts to make friends again, was never entirely forgiven; George seems to have inherited some of his father's rancour. Relations were still cold when George won the prize for the Greek Ode at Cambridge, and Southey wrote to Bedford: 'I felt five minutes inclination to write and congratulate him—but five minutes reflection prevented me.'

Nevertheless when he heard in 1798 that George was leaving for India he wrote warmly to him. 'Bath: May 11th 1798. My dear Strachey; I learn from Wynn that you are shortly about to quit the kingdom, so shortly indeed that I shall not see you before your departure, but you must not go without receiving my wishes for your welfare. Little intimate as we have been of late years, I have always thought of you with affection—and I feel now that I am losing a friend. I have desired Cottle to forward my book to you immediately, it will not occupy much room in your baggage, and it may sometimes remind you of one who will often think of you as his earliest friend. God bless you, Strachey, and may you return from India with as uncorrupted a heart as you will carry there! Yours truly and affectionately, Robert Southey.'

He also wrote a sonnet in his honour.

> Fair be thy fortunes in the distant land,
> Companion of my earlier years and friend!
> Go to the Eastern world, and may the hand
> Of Heaven its blessings on thy labour send.
> And may I, if we ever more should meet,
> See thee with affluence to thy native shore
> Return'd. I need not pray that I may greet

The same untainted goodness as before.
Long years must intervene before that day;
And what the changes Heaven to each may send,
It boots not now to bode: O early friend!
Assured no distance e'er can wear away
Esteem long rooted, and no change remove
The dear remembrance of the friend we love.

George spent over twenty years in India, and finally became Chief Secretary of the Company in Madras, though unlike most Stracheys it appears that he never really enjoyed the life or the country. As Southey wrote to a mutual friend: 'I am sorry Strachey is so disgusted with India, though I cannot wish he were otherwise. From all accounts an English East Indian is a very bad animal: they have adopted by force the luxury of the country, and its tyranny and pride by choice. A man who thinks and feels must be in solitude there.'

While George was in India there were no fewer than five young Stracheys there at once, all of nearly the same age: George and his brother John, and Sir Henry's three sons, Henry, Edward and Richard.

Southey was always urging George to marry and deplored his life-long bachelorhood, feeling that he was 'made for domestic life', but one can't help wondering if he was entirely right in his assessment of George's domestic suitability, as he seems to have been a somewhat morose and unsociable man.

In the end, however, Southey began to give up. In 1805 he wrote to William Wynn:

I have written to him, and twice sent him books to India, he has never written me a line. The truth of the matter is this. At one time he thought it prudent to drop his acquaintance with me but the recollection which he had of old times, and the feeling which he had towards me in the bottom of his heart and the connecting link which you formed forced him to an occasional intercourse which was always uncomfortable and which I ought to have broken off seeing that his father passed me in the streets. Strachey feels all this, and when he remembers me he is not pleased with himself because he knows he has acted inconsistently, less unkindly than he meant to have acted— more so than he ought. . . . I will not therefore write to him again, nor in any way force myself upon him. When he returns to England if we should meet by chance, as most probably we shall, I shall not forget his very many very excellent qualities, nor the deep and uneffaced prepossession in his favour which I felt the very first day I ever saw him, when I was placed under his shadow.

When George finally returned to England in 1820, Southey still nourished hopes of a reconciliation, but nothing much seems to have come of them. 'George Strachey is arrived and we have called upon each other,' he reported to his wife, 'but have not yet met.' And later the same year: 'I dined with Bedford where I shall meet Wynn and probably my old schoolfellow, George Strachey.'

It sounds as though even Southey's emotional warmth had been dampened in the end by George's cool neglect.

The Archdeacon, despite his ten children, had only one surviving Strachey grandson, and his brother Sir Henry's line, even thought it was less prolific to start with, produced more Stracheys in the end.

Sir Henry's eldest son and heir, the second Sir Henry, however, never married. Born in 1772, he too went to Westminster, a few years earlier than George, and later to Edinburgh University. He was appointed a Writer to the Company, went to India and became a Judge. Although he did not stay in India very long, but resigned and returned to England in 1805, five years before his father died, his service appears to have been sufficiently distinguished for John Mill, father of John Stuart Mill, to praise him on a number of occasions in his history of India, calling him 'an excellent magistrate and one of the most respectable of Indian judges'. No doubt this praise was in part due however, to the fact that Henry shared Mill's Utilitarian views.

Young Henry's opinions were, in fact, extremely radical. His father had wanted him to stay at home and follow him into politics, but Henry had become a convinced Radical at

Edinburgh, as well as developing a general distaste for the current practice of politics. The older Henry was, although not, as he said himself, 'a Party man', yet more or less a Tory of a moderate kind, and young Henry, being personally very fond of his father, was unhappy at the thought of having to vote against him in Parliament, particularly as Sir Henry was a member of the Government. He also strongly disapproved of the purchase of Parliamentary seats, and although his mother offered to buy one for him for £4,000 when he left India, he declined. Ideas and morality in politics, as elsewhere, were changing fast.

When he first inherited Sutton Court, Henry, like his father, spent little time there, but by the age of 40 he had settled down sufficiently to become High Sheriff of Somerset, though he always preferred Rook's Nest, the house his father had inherited in Surrey.

All his life he was not only a confirmed Utilitarian but a complete sceptic of the school of Hume and Gibbon; entirely scornful of what he deemed 'superstition'. He once told his nephew that he had not supposed that any thinking man believed in Christianity until his fellow Whig, the witty parson Sidney Smith, one day told him that there were such believers. Henry added, however: 'He did not say that he himself believed it.'

He was a complete, dry intellectual, too, devoted to the study of Persian and European literature and history, but entirely without imagination, appreciating Shakespeare purely for his intellect, not his feeling or poetry. He had little love for the visual arts or the aesthetic side of history, and no patience with the contemporary craze for 'medievalism', allowing the estate mason to mix mortar in the Cromwellian breastplate inherited from the Hodges, and destroying some of the manor's oldest features. His family, however, found him kindly and hospitable, if extremely eccentric, increasingly so in old age.

Finally his mind began to give way in patches. His nephew John, in 1857, said that he had 'very little mind left, but that little was pretty rational'. He was still sane enough, for instance, to be furious with his nephew Edward for writing a book about miracles.

He was too rational, in fact, for doctors to declare him unfit to

manage his affairs and this had become desirable because he had
engaged a sinister couple called Harris as housekeeper and agent.
They were threatening to cut down all the timber on the estate
and marry Henry off (although he was well over 80) to a niece of
theirs. They drafted a new Will for him leaving everything to
them, but mercifully he died before they had managed to get him
to sign it. John came to Sutton Court to sort things out and the
Harrises fled to America, with their son, taking with them a lot of
the first Sir Henry's papers, which they sold on arrival.

Like so many Stracheys, Henry had made literary friends,
notably Walter Savage Landor, normally famous for his quarrel-
some nature, with whom he continued to maintain friendly
relations until he died in 1858. The previous year Landor wrote to
Henry, 'I hope to spend another day with you at Sutton Court. A
few poems of mine are about to be published. I make a present of
them to Nichols of Edinborough—for I never wish to profit by
anything I write or do. I was incited to this publication that I
might record, for another generation or two, my esteem of Sir
Henry Strachey.'

The resulting poem, written in the heat of the reaction to the
Indian Mutiny, read as follows:

To Sir Henry Strachey.

Strachey! now mays't thou praise thy God
That thy tired feet long since retrod
Thy ancient hall, thy native fields,
And spurned the wealth that India yields.
Millions were grateful for thy care,
For wrong redressed and guilt laid bare;
Shortlived is gratitude, of all
The Virtues first to faint and fall.
The court where thy tribunal stood
Is dyed and drench't with British Blood.
Mothers and infants lie around
Hewn piecemeal; but from one worse wound
Brave husbands save a fond chaste breast,
Pierce it, and there again find rest.

If Henry lived long enough to read this in one of his saner moments, despite his friendship with the author one can imagine the scorn with which he would have greeted its fustian sentiments.

Henry = Jane Latham
1st Baronet   (b. Kelsall)
1736–1810   1738–1824

Charlotte
1771–1801
d. unm.

Henry
2nd Baronet
1772–1858
d. unm.

Edward
1774–1832
see TREE 8

Richard
of Ashwick
Grove
1781–1847

= Anne Maria
Powell
m.1830

Lucy = Col F. Wollaston
b.1782
no children

Georgiana m.1847 d.1847
= George
Strachey
see TREE 7

Charlotte
= John James
Phillipps
('Uncle Beau')
see TREE 6

Richard
b.1835
Descendants
in New Zealand

Henry

Alexander

4 daughters

Isabella
= John H. Baker
explorer in
New Zealand

FAMILY TREE 5

'THE ENGLISH ADONIS' IN PERSIA

Richard Strachey

(1781–1847)

Sir Henry the elder is shown in his portraits wearing powdered hair, while the younger Henry had grey hair and piercing hazel eyes. The two younger brothers, however, Edward and Richard had large lustrous black eyes, fine bones and coal black hair. This dominant genetic inheritance, which persisted for several generations, is not apparent in the portrait of the John Strachey of the Stuart period, who clearly had fair hair and blue eyes. It is interesting—if fruitless—to try to guess whence it came. There is, so far as one can see, no chance that it came from Indian blood, though both Edward and Richard had an Indian look. Perhaps Sir Henry's mother, Helen Clerk of Edinburgh, was what is sometimes called 'a Black Celt'.

This romantic oriental appearance, however, helped to influence the career of the younger brother, Richard. Born in 1781, and a godson of Lord Howe, cheerful and adventurous in character, he duly followed the family tradition and became a Writer in the Company's service when he was seventeen. Less than two years later an English mission was planned, to be led by Captain John Malcolm, later Sir John and a great name in the history of British India who had been appointed Envoy to Persia, and became a lifelong friend both of Richard and of his brothers.

Malcolm was to go to the ruler, Fath Ali Shah, and endeavour to persuade him to ally his country with Britain rather than with Napoleon, whose progress in Egypt was causing the British considerable alarm, lest he should follow the example of Alexander the Great and try to conquer India.

Richard, as soon as he heard of this plan, was eager to join Malcolm's party, and his superior in Madras, the second Lord Clive, who had been the ward of Richard's father, agreed to let him go and wrote reassuringly to Sir Henry that it was what he would have done for his own son.

Malcolm's 'family' or staff consisted of six men: three assistants, of whom Richard was one, the Commander of the Escort, a surgeon and a secretary, while at their first stop, Muscat, they picked up a second surgeon.

The party sailed from Bombay at the end of 1799 for Muscat, where Malcolm formed a high opinion of the ruler, and signed a valuable commercial treaty with him. He also introduced the 'Irish' potato into the country, where it flourished and was known as 'Malcolm's plum'.

Richard, full of excitement, wrote to his father:

I shall be glad to hear what you think of my expedition to Persia. I little thought a few months ago that I should date a letter to you on 9th January 1800 from Arabia. You will no doubt be very glad to hear that I am become a such a great Traveller. I have seen more of India than most people of my standing, and I think I shall acquire a good deal more knowledge by being with this Embassy than remaining at Calcutta.' He went on to describe Muscat. 'There are two or three forts towards the bay, but they are in such a state that they hardly deserve the name. The town has a wall round it, with a few bastions which would most likely give way if a gun was fired from them. The Bazar streets have a very singular appearance. They are mostly covered at top, and are very narrow. The whole while I was in them, I could not help thinking I was in a house.'

Ormuz, where they went next, he found a very barren and salty place.

The party then furnished itself with horses, which Richard found both more spirited and gentler than those to be found in India, and pressed on to Shiraz.

Persians at that time had had very few contacts with Europeans, and the last English Envoy had been in the days of Queen Elizabeth, so the party attracted much attention.

Richard was much impressed by what he saw, and when the party reached Kazeroon in June he wrote:

We have already passed some of the most tremendous mountains it is possible to conceive, however we hear that they are nothing to what we have before us. The thermometer is now near 100, yet we have as much snow as we please. The town here is large, but I should not think it populous, a great part of it is apparently in ruins, and it has been plundered several times in the course of the wars and troubles which are continually ravaging this country. The Governor is an old man, who with one of his sons, had his eyes put out a few years since, but this is nothing extraordinary in Persia.

The thought of the violence clearly appealed to the schoolboy in him as he wrote again about it to his sister Charlotte. 'This is an extraordinary country, neither like India nor England, in either its appearance or Inhabitants. They are always fighting with their neighbours or among themselves. With regard to putting out eyes and cutting off ears, three or four hundred pair of each in a crack are reckoned nothing in Persia.'

Despite his own preference for informality, Malcolm soon realized that in Persia it was essential to obey strict protocol if one did not wish to be utterly despised. Such things as the order in which coffee was served, or the height at which one's chair was placed, were vital, and the Envoy had to protest with fierce dignity when efforts were made by his Persian hosts to test him by surreptitiously downgrading his status. He won this battle in the end, and when the party arrived before Shiraz there was much exchanging of gifts, hunting expeditions and feasting, seated on what Malcolm called 'a haystack of rose petals'.

When they entered the city there was a splendid and colourful welcome. 'On our flank rode the Mehmandar, or Entertainer, with his Attendants', wrote Richard,

He is an Omrah of high Rank, deputed from the Shah Zadeh, or Prince, according to Persian custom, to conduct the Embassy. . . . After we had proceeded about a mile, we were met by

Nasuroolla Khaun Karagoozaloo, Commander in chief of all the forces in Fars. . . . and several other Omrahs, attended by a thousand Horse. They accompanied us to our tents where they were treated with Coffee and Sherbet and Kullians [apparatus for smoking]. They remained about an hour and then departed, much gratified, I suppose, by having seen so many beings of a kind they never before beheld and hardly ever heard of.

They pushed on from Shiraz to Isfahan, stopping at the ruins of Persepolis on the way. Richard, unlike most of the party, was deeply interested and, in the predatory fashion of the day, hunted for treasure trove. 'I wished much', he wrote to his father, 'to bring away with me some specimens of the carved figures etc on the walls. The whole edifice, however, being black granite, no tool could make an impression. I also dug with pickaxes etc in several places, but had only the luck to meet with a profile (basso rilievo) of an old man's head, with a curiously curled beard and hair, which I have preserved very carefully.'

Malcolm, too, was fascinated by the mysterious ruined palace, but others of the party were more interested in the duck-shooting.

Richard's younger sister, Lucy, was just eighteen, but she had three brothers and two cousins in India at the time, and was naturally expected to take an interest in all things oriental. 'This is a fine place,' Richard wrote to her, 'as you may perhaps often have heard. . . . We at present occupy a garden about a mile from the city, called Jehan Nimau (or A Pattern of the World); any Persian scholar will tell you what a fine place it must be when you say that it is on the scite [sic] of old Jafferabad, and that the stream of Raknabad runs through it, that the tomb of the immortal Haufiz is not five hundred yards from it.'

Aware, however, that Lucy might have other interests, he adds kindly: 'I am glad to hear that you are learning to play on the guitar,' and offers to send her some of the mosquitoes flying round his legs if he can catch them. He also replies to some of her questions: 'Tygers and lions are in abundance, however I have seen none but tame ones. . . . With regard to spitting in Brazen

Machines, those who are rich use silver ones, and as to Betel there is none, I believe, in Persia . . . with respect to putting on my own stockings, I always do it when I am not lazy. You ask how I like the black servants; some are very good, and a great many superlative rascals. The Persians make pretty good servants, but they are not black.'

For his mother he had a number of schoolboy requests; for seals with his crest and motto, and a new coat, and a complaint that his father had been writing about his affairs to his high-level friends in India. 'I cannot here help again saying what a mistake my Father has made. I have to beg that he will never write to the Government again about my allowances. India is not like what it was formerly, or my Father must have forgotten what the Governor General is.'

'Persians,' said Malcolm, 'are more than goodlooking, they are a handsome race of men.' They put a high value on beauty, and he knew that the appearance of his party was of no little importance. Indeed it was partly on account of his dark good looks that Richard had been chosen. He was clean-shaven and richly dressed, and his face and figure made such an impression that he was known as the Persian equivalent of the English Adonis, and became a byword for beauty. A number of miniatures were painted of him, and hung in various palaces of the Shah, and his portrait appeared on all sorts of objects such as pipes and pen cases. When the then Shah visited London seventy years later, the wife of another Richard Strachey met one of his suite, who, on hearing her name exclaimed 'Ah! Ystrenche!' and told her that the name was still associated with good looks in his country. Lord Curzon in his book *Persia and the Persian Question*, published in 1892, reported that Fath Ali Shah, the Persian ruler at the time of the mission, and an accomplished poet, had himself written an ode to Richard, and had hung his portrait between two legendary heroes on the wall of the Kasr-i-Kajar palace. The whole story, too, is still remembered by Persian scholars to this day.

When the travellers finally arrived in Teheran, the seat of the Shah, they made an impressive entry into the royal presence. All the servants were dressed in silk or cloth tunics, with new lambswool caps. They were all (says Malcolm) scrupulously clean, their heads were shaved and their beards trimmed. There were nine splendidly dressed grooms leading beautiful horses, followed by eight footmen. Then came the Envoy and his suite, followed by a large cavalry escort with trumpets and kettle-drums.

Among the many presents brought for the Shah, the most welcome, not surprisingly perhaps, in that beauty-conscious country, were a number of huge pier glasses, which had caused endless trouble to transport.

If the Embassy impressed the Persians, so did their hosts impress them. 'Yesterday we had our first audience with the King,' wrote Richard to his father: 'the whole of which was the grandest sight I ever beheld. . . . Nothing could exceed the richness of the King's dress, his jewels alone were worth upwards of a million sterling, and the Masnad* upon which he sat was of red velvet adorned with pearls . . . in short the whole sight could not possibly be exceeded by any kind of magnificence.'

There was one present that Richard sent home which was of a kind to appeal particularly to his family. 'The cats here,' he wrote to Lucy, 'are very fine, with long hair and bushy tails. I shall accordingly not fail in sending a specimen of them to Hill Street.'

The mission succeeded, and the Shah happily agreed to sign two treaties, one commercial, providing for the establishment of British 'factories' in Persia, and the other political. Unfortunately shifting alliances among the various powers, France, Britain and Russia, caused the Shah to turn to the French in 1805, and it was not until a second mission was sent in 1809 that the French were finally outmanoeuvred.

Following this adventure Richard acted for some time as assistant in the Persian Secretary's office in Calcutta. He was posted to England in 1803, and returned to India three years later overland, via St Petersburg, Moscow, the Caucasus and Turkey, taking seven months over the journey.

This too was a considerable adventure, and Richard now 25, with his friend Capper and his favourite dog, Glancer, travelled from Elsinore—where he was forbidden access to the battle-

---

* Throne.

ments, and thus 'lost the chance of scraping acquaintance with the Ghost'.

Despite the continuing war with France there was almost no fear of meeting enemy ships. 'A French vessel', he wrote, 'has not been seen in these seas for a very long period and the Prussian ports are blockaded by the Swedes.'

They went on to St Petersburg and were given much conflicting advice on the safest route to take. They finally decided to make for a place called Mosdok, at the foot of the Caucasus, and thence to the passes and Tiflis.

By August 1806 Richard reported that he had reached Moscow, noting that the road from St Petersburg was 'the best he had ever seen, being made of very thick boards'. It was out of season in Moscow and there was little in the way of social life, so they pushed on as fast as possible, riding twelve to eighteen hours a day and picking up local guides and costume as they went.

At first the country seemed fairly prosperous, with many wagons drawn by oxen taking goods to the Crimea in return for salt; the roads not made, but good; the winds hot and strong and the fleas 'immense'.

They passed through towns where people lived permanently on upper floors because of constant floods, and where excellent melons were to be found. Here, in Cossack country, Glancer was lost, but Richard went back for him on foot—seven versts*— found him and was given a lucky lift back by two Russian officers. A little later he also lost his passport, which would have been a disaster, but that he found that too, on retracing his steps.

When they reached the Caucasus they were most hospitably treated by the General in Command, and given passes and escorts as far as Tiflis and the frontier.

Conditions had become bad. 'This place is . . . execrable,' he wrote to his cousin Charles Kelsall. 'Not only the sun but plague, pestilence and almost famine. The country is full of quarantine stations and as a particular favour I understand that we shall be permitted to go out of it after having been well fumigated.'

---

* Nearly five miles.

They crossed the Caucasus without mishap and reached Tiflis, where they were advised to avoid Persia, 'for besides the war between the Persians and Russians, the former are now at war with the Pashaw of Baghdad.' So they decided to travel through Turkey instead.

Here the roads were considered dangerous, and they were forced into many diversions on their way to Baghdad. Richard was, however, undeterred. 'I have not yet repented my journey by land,' he wrote, 'and am determined never to return to England by sea, so much do I prefer the former. It will not, however, be very difficult to find an easier and better route than this. But I have already, in the course of this journey, seen and learned more probably than I could elsewhere of things which occur not daily in the course of this life.'

Unfortunately Richard's companion became dangerously ill of a fever at this stage, and had to be carried in a litter. However he recovered gradually, especially when they reached the Tigris and were able to proceed more comfortably by boat. Despite attacks by wandering tribes of Kurds they succeeded in reaching Baghdad, and finally India.

Still eager to see and experience everything, the following year Richard joined another hazardous and important mission, this time to Kabul, with his brother's friend Elphinstone.

Richard was sociable and popular, as Elphinstone testified. He was Resident at Gwalior later, where he had to cope with the tricky Maharajah Scindia, who was turning a deliberately blind eye to the raids made by his subjects on the neighbouring British-protected state of Bhopal. Richard wrote to his friend John Adam, Political Secretary to the Governor, sending a private letter with every official despatch. In June 1813 he wrote: 'The anarchy of a great part of Gwalior to which my official letter to you of this date principally relates, may, from the nature of the country and the total want of Police, be more than Sindeah can easily remedy. But no consideration of the faults of his Administration can be allowed in excuse for hostile attacks of his troops.' Adam wrote back: 'Your account of Sindeah's military force will be highly useful. I have no fear with respect to his regular forces, but the means he will have of letting loose the Pindarries on our defenceless provinces is very alarming and renders the gaining of time an object of peculiar importance.'

By 1815 things had quietened down, and Richard was able to write: 'All is quiet here (Mahratta tranquillity—comparative, of course). Bhopaul is hardly ever mentioned at the Durbar. The Maharajah is busy fishing, shooting, hunting and in other outdoor pastimes; his Ministers marrying, amusements eminently suitable to the happy enjoyment of a Gwalior summer.'

Richard's own enjoyment was marred by the death of his beloved hound Glancer. He was buried in great splendour in a circular tomb with eight pillars, containing a memorial poem, one verse of which read:

> How graceful hang thy ears: what varied guise
> Adorned thy coat so sleek.
> But who shall paint thy full expressive eyes,
> Those eyes that seemed to speak.

They were indeed painted, and a speaking likeness of Glancer used to hang in the house Richard bought on his retirement, near Sutton Court, called Ashwick Grove.

Richard's health was inevitably beginning to suffer from the climate, and he wrote to Adam during the summer of 1815: 'I am still confined by my Eye, which has produced a Boil on the lid, and is *bunged* in consequence.' He was moved to Lucknow in the north, but was slow to recover and spent much time and energy trying to reclaim his expenses from the Government. 'I have a headache and a bad eye into the bargain', he wrote to Adam in February 1816, 'so you will excuse this short answer. Owing you the burden of writing on this by no means amusing matter has been my fault by not waiting and having the discussion with the Department of Audits.'

On the way to Lucknow, however, he had been able to stop over in Agra, where he could see the Taj Mahal from his window. 'I couldn't resist going to it last night,' he told Adam. 'I found it to the full as enchanting as we left it. You would have enjoyed a second pilgrimage to it highly.'

He returned to England for good in 1817 at 36, but did not

marry until 1830, when he was 49. He then had two sons and six daughters and died in 1847. His descendants inherited his looks, and the Ashwick Grove Stracheys long had a reputation for being handsome.

There was a close and continuing friendship between Richard's branch and the descendants of his brother Edward; one of his daughters, Georgiana, married Edward's youngest son, George, and another married the only son of the romantic Kitty Kirkpatrick, whose cousin Julia, Edward had married.

WITH THE KIRKPATRICKS IN INDIA

Edward Strachey

(1774–1808)

Edward, Sir Henry's second son—the boy with the intelligent black eyes—was born in 1774 and went out to India in his turn as a Company Writer. He had been educated, in the family tradition, at Westminster school, and then went on to St Andrew's University, in Scotland. There he learned to play the flute, among other things, and to enjoy mathematics and golf—even cutting up the scarlet academic gown which was (and is) a feature of St Andrews, to make a golfing coat.

He was a small dark man with a sharp nose; his mother Jenny had been heavily pregnant at the time of Clive's suicide, and when Edward was born with a red mark on his forehead, she attributed this, in accordance with the beliefs of the day, to her having seen Clive covered in his blood.

He was nineteen when he arrived in India. At that time there were no aptitude tests or examinations for young Writers, but they were required to sign a list of rules and a covenant with the Company. To the great astonishment of the officials, Edward refused to sign without reading both documents carefully, a thing which had apparently never happened before.

In those days the boys who arrived as Writers were still often ill educated and untrained, and little was done to help them when they started work, so that they often took to drink and gambling, ran into debt and turned to illicit trading to recoup.

Edward was too rational a creature to be misled in this way, and was encouraged by the example of Lord Cornwallis, the same man who had been a general in the American War; a man of sterling character and integrity, who was Governor General when Edward first came out, and was doing what he could to improve matters.

By 1798 Edward had acquired a good knowledge of Persian

? 1. = Col James Kirkpatrick = 2. Katherine Munro
       The Handsome Colonel   b.1743 m.1762
       1729-1818

Mary Pawson = Brig. William
              1754-1812

George = ?   Lt Col James Achilles = Khair
b.1763   1704-1805   un Nissa

James   John   3 daughters   William = Cassie ?   Kitty   = Capt James
                                     1801-28   1802-89   Winsloe
                                                                     Phillipps

Clementina   Barbara   Julia   Elizabeth
= Admiral   = Charles   1790-1846   d. unm.
Lord Louis   Buller MP   = Edward
                             Strachey
                             1774-1832
                             see TREES 7, 8 & 9

Charles   Arthur
MP   judge in India

3 daughters   John James   = Charlotte
               ('Uncle Beau') Strachey
                               niece of Edward
                               see TREE 5

FAMILY TREE 6

and Hindi and had made particular friends with a young man called Mountstuart Elphinstone, some five years younger than he, with whom he shared lodgings. He had also made good friends with a more senior character, some twenty years older, Major General William Kirkpatrick, who was at that time Political Secretary to the Governor General, Lord Wellesley, and whose daughter Julia he later married. This started a connection between the Strachey and Kirkpatrick families which was to last for several generations.

William Kirkpatrick was a brilliant scholar and linguist, with a rare knowledge of Asian literature, social customs and traditions and great fluency in Persian. He had been sent on a mission to Nepal—the first Englishman to reach Nayakote where the Nepalese rajahs held court—and had written a book about the country. He had also been for some years Resident at the court of the Nizam of Hyderabad, the huge and important state in the Deccan for whose alliance the French and the English were competing.

The British were more or less in control in the north of India, but the situation in the south was still both chaotic and dangerous, and was the scene of constant three-sided warfare between Hyderabad, Mysore, under the warlike Tippoo Sultan, and the equally warlike Mahratta Confederation based on Poona in the south-west—a struggle in which both the British and the French were inevitably involved.

Tippoo was a soldier rather than an aristocrat; he had offered the Nizam an alliance against the Mahrattas in 1787, but his terms were refused as they included a marriage with one of Tippoo's relations, which the Nizam regarded as degrading. He did not, in any case, wish to commit himself completely to Tippoo, and sought European alliances instead.

Meanwhile Cornwallis had been succeeded as Governor General by Sir John Shore, who obediently followed the Company's orders to avoid involvement in native wars and to preserve neutrality in the interests of economy. This drove the Nizam to the French, and he engaged a Frenchman called Michel Joachim Raymond, a highly efficient mercenary, to raise and lead a force in Hyderabad.

In 1795 the fighting culminated—through no fault of Raymond's—in a disgraceful defeat of the Nizam's troops by the Mahrattas at Khadia. Members of the Nizam's extensive harem, it was claimed, had joined him on the field, and half-way through the battle took flight in panic, followed first by the Nizam himself and then by the whole army.

The Nizam's Wazir, Aristojah, and his Commander, Mir Alum, both favoured a British rather than a French alliance, and Mir Alum was sent to Calcutta as Minister for English affairs. After the defeat, however, Aristojah was forced to spend two years in the Mahratta capital, Poona, as a hostage, and French counsels tended to prevail.

Later that year, 1795, one of the Nizam's sons rose in revolt, and his father sought help from both the French and the British. Alarmed by Kirkpatrick's report of Raymond's growing influence and revolutionary politics, Shore finally agreed to send in British troops, but the French were already on the spot, and the British arrived too late to share in the credit for suppressing the revolt.

Though he was only 43, William's health was deteriorating, and in 1797 he was forced to sail for Cape Town on sick leave, leaving his younger brother, Captain James Achilles Kirkpatrick, who had been his Assistant, as Acting Resident. In Cape Town he met Lord Wellesley, on his way to succeed the pusillanimous Shore as Governor General.

Richard Wellesley was a very different character from Shore. He was the eldest of a very talented set of brothers, of whom one was to become Lord Wellington. He was extremely intelligent, able, determined and energetic. He was also extremely arrogant, and so little in favour of the Company policy of neutralism that he ignored it completely. His Empire-building tendencies and their mounting cost finally led to his recall and attack in Parliament, but not before he and his brother Arthur had achieved a number of military and political successes.

On his way out to India Wellesley took the opportunity of consulting Kirkpatrick on the Indian situation in general and on the particular urgency of affairs in Hyderabad, and found his advice invaluable, as he reported later.

'In the Cape,' he wrote, 'where he [Kirkpatrick] had gone for recovery of his health, I put some questions to him relative to the French influence in Hyderabad, which he answered with much clearness. I desired him to put my queries and his replies on paper, which he did in a way that *delighted* me. These communications joined to the common impression of his character and talents, introduced him to my Family [Wellesley's staff] without any other recommendation.'

The war with France was at its height in Europe, a consideration which overshadowed British policy all over the world for many years. 'I determined to overthrow the French influence at Hyderabad', Wellesley went on, 'and that important object was happily and speedily accomplished in the ablest manner.'

Wellesley arrived in Calcutta in late May 1798, and before the end of July he had appointed William to his staff and later as Political Secretary to the Government, while he himself was already in close and detailed correspondence with the young James Achilles, the Acting Resident in Hyderabad, on the terms of the vital Treaty he planned for the Nizam.

James Achilles was handsome and munificent, a man with a genuine love of the Oriental way of life. He enjoyed hunting, hawking, cock and partridge fighting, made friends easily with the Indians, and took with enthusiasm to the colourful Oriental pomp and splendour of the court, often wearing Indian clothes when not on duty. He was greatly liked by the Nizam, who on 9th February 1798 had issued a Firman (which is still to be seen in the official Archives in Hyderabad) bestowing on him several titles, including that of Nawab Hashmat Jang Bahadur, meaning Glorious in Battle.

By this time Raymond had raised 15,000 good troops in Hyderabad and was in a position of great power in the state. James Achilles, however, was an able negotiator, and in March 1798 Raymond died; some say 'suddenly' after himself poisoning his favourite horse and hound, some say after a long illness. Whatever the cause, his death was extremely advantageous to the English, as his successor, Piron, was a crude, inferior man, and not popular. Raymond, on the other hand, was much liked; he was known locally as Mizarem, and an annual fair with illuminations was celebrated in his honour until late in the following century.

The treaty which Kirkpatrick was instructed to conclude with the Nizam was the first of an important series of 'Subsidiary Treaties' with independent Princes by which the British would finally achieve effective control of almost the whole subcontinent. In return for British protection it called for the immediate disbandment of the French troops and the promise not to go to war or to make alliances with neighbouring states without consulting the British. A British troop was to be formed instead of the French, paid for by the Nizam either in cash or territory ceded to the British. Advised by both Aristojah (now returned from Poona) and Mir Alum, the Nizam duly signed in September 1798, but continued to delay week after week in actually disbanding the French troops, as promised. James Achilles was forced to threaten to attack them, in spite of the danger of widespread bloodshed and of causing the men to abscond with their guns and go over to Tippoo.

When the Nizam did finally give the order to disband, and the French officers relayed it to the troops, the men rose against the officers and imprisoned them. James Achilles, with the young John Malcolm, who had been appointed his assistant, and Colonel Roberts, commanding his troops, acted with great speed and resolution. They surrounded the French camp and threatened to shoot if the officers were not surrendered and all arms laid down. Some of the Indian troops, who had served under the popular Malcolm, recognized him; the surrender was peacefully accomplished and the whole troop disarmed and disbanded without a shot being fired. No one could have hoped for so complete and masterly a stroke, and the whole affair had a considerable effect in other parts of India.

Wellesley was delighted. Indeed he had cause to be, as the Company granted him £500 a year for twenty years as a reward for what James Achilles had done. He wrote: 'I am happy to express my entire approbation of the judgment, firmness and discretion you have manifested.' He put James Achilles forward to the Government for a Baronetcy, but nothing was done for him or for several others whom Wellesley had recommended.

Left: Richard
Strachey
(1781–1847).
Persian miniature

Right: Fath Ali
Shah, Ruler of
Persia in 1800

Above left: Khair un Nissa, wife of James Achilles Kirkpatrick
Above right: James Achilles Kirkpatrick (1764-1805), Artist unknown
Below left: William Kirkpatrick (1801-28), Artist unknown
Below right: Nizam Khan Asaf Jah II of Hyderabad

The Kirkpatrick children, William and Kitty, by George Chinnery, 1805

The Residency
at Hyderabad

William Kirkpatrick, indeed, was dismissed from his post as Political Secretary by order of the Directors of the Company.

Wellesley took this as a personal affront and complained: 'All these persons I had recommended in the strongest terms to the Government of India at home. Nor to this hour can I divine a rational motive for the treatment which these valuable characters have experienced excepting it be a latent jealousy of my success and a secret desire to suppress every character and circumstance which could render its lustre more distinguished.'

Meanwhile James Achilles, now officially confirmed as Resident, had become deeply involved in his own private affairs. The court at Hyderabad was Mohammedan, and no mixing with the ladies was possible, but it was not impossible for the invisible ones to look down from their latticed balconies and observe the ceremonies and those who took part in them. A cousin of Mir Alum called Akil ud Dowlah, the Nizam's Paymaster General, had a very beautiful young granddaughter, Khair un Nissa (meaning Excellent among Women). How she first saw James Achilles cannot now be determined, but when she did she fell violently and permanently in love with him.

She sent an old woman servant to the Residency, (As James told his brother William in a letter), to tell him of her mistress's love and to ask for his in return. James refused, but the messenger came again several times, always to be sent away. Finally one evening as he sat alone in the house, Khair un Nissa herself, veiled and alone, entered the room.

On the first occasion James Achilles was able to resist even this. At this meeting, he wrote,

I contrived to command myself so far as to abstain from the tempting feast I was manifestly invited to, and though God knows but ill qualified for the task, attempted to argue this romantic young creature out of a passion which I could not, I confess, help myself feeling something more than pity for. She declared to me again and again that her affections had been irrevocably fixed on me for a series of time, that her Fate was linked to mine and that she would be content to pass her days with me as the humblest of handmaidens. . . . Until the above time the young lady's person was inviolate, but was it in human nature to remain proof against another such fiery trial? . . . The grandfather and the mother, (though they kept aloof on the occasion) were privy to the assignation.

A few days later James was summoned to her grandmother in the women's quarters, the *zenana*. The girl had, they told him, already attempted to poison herself, and would do so again if he did not grant her plea. 'I went there', he wrote,

and when I assure you, which I do most solemnly—that the grandmother herself initiated the design of this meeting, and the granddaughter, in faint and broken accents, hinted that my listening to her suit was the only chance (as she fondly persuaded herself) of avoiding a hateful marriage, I think you cannot but allow that I must have been something more or less than man to have held out any longer. . . . Deliberate female seduction I hold in as much contempt and detestation as any man . . . but I can on no account endure the slightest whisper of its having been either dishonourable or ungenerous.

All Khair un Nissa's family, however, were not equally in favour of the match. Her father, Mahmood Ali Khan, had perished in a gun accident not long before, and her paternal grandfather, Bajar Ali Khan, together with the women of the family, all approved, but her maternal grandfather, Akil ud Dowlah, was violently opposed. He complained to his cousin, Mir Alum, who had fallen out of favour with the Nizam owing to the jealousy of the Wazir and had been banished from the capital. Mir Alum had a grudge against Kirkpatrick for refusing to accept a bribe he had offered, and he was delighted to use his cousin's complaints to further his own cause. . . . He wrote to the Governor General on 18th February 1800, telling him of the affair and claiming that it was causing great scandal, and that Kirkpatrick had forced the girl. He also claimed that Kirkpatrick was responsible for his own [Mir Alum's] disgrace and that gossip had linked the Resident with the murder of Mahmood Ali Khan, Khair un Nissa's father.

All this, he said, had given him 'the greatest degree of grief and concern, for whilst the public talk upon the subject of the first accusation of the murder of Mahmood Ali Khan remains yet unstifled, should the second circumstance, that of the marriage, take place, the public will obtain an extraordinary handle of conversation and the former accusation will receive general credit.'

Lord Wellesley was not pleased. He discounted the murder accusation, but there was always some official disapproval when Englishmen became involved with high-class Indian ladies, for fear that political pressure might be brought to bear on them, and Wellesley himself was more prejudiced on the subject of race and mixed marriages than his predecessors had been. He had, for instance, banned all Indians and those of mixed parentage from the Governor's hospitality.

He circulated the letter round his Council and wrote to Hyderabad to demand an instant enquiry. His correspondence with the Resident concerning the two further treaties to be agreed with the Nizam suddenly became very testy in tone and James Achilles was reprimanded first for softness and then for arrogance.

When the local enquiry demanded by the Governor General took place, it cleared Kirkpatrick completely, but Wellesley remained displeased.

Meanwhile, to counter local gossip, James Achilles decided to marry Khair un Nissa according to the Muslim rite. To do this, however, he would have—at least nominally—to convert to Islam, as although Muslim men were allowed to marry Christian women, Muslim women might only marry Muslims. He very probably agreed to do this, though there is no direct evidence other than a letter in which he claimed that his conduct throughout the business had been 'totally free of aught of a tendency to arouse or outrage their religious prejudices'.

The Nizam, in any case, adopted James as his son and undertook to stand as his father at the ceremony, while the Wazir was to stand as father of the bride. The Nizam's ladies then visited Khair un Nissa's mother, whereupon Akil ud Dowlah, who was present, became enraged, drew his sword and threatened his own daughter and her guests. The Nizam called him an idiot and said he deserved prison or banishment; he was forced to give way, and the wedding took place.

In due course news of all these events reached Colonel Arthur Wellesley, (later Lord Wellington) engaged in clearing up operations near Mysore, after the fall of Seringapatam and the death of Tippoo Sultan. Arthur Wellesley had no great sympathy with Mir Alum, but he greatly disliked James Achilles Kirkpatrick for what he called his 'pompous and overbearing behaviour' and felt that the Resident had been an idiot to allow himself to be used as a political pawn.

He wrote to Colonel Close, the Resident in Mysore, about the whole Hyderabad position in September 1800, by which time Khair un Nissa was pregnant, mockingly referring to James Achilles from time to time as Hashmat Jang—the Glorious in War.

'Mir Alum complains of our friends at Hyderabad most bitterly', he wrote.

It appears to me from all that I have heard, that Aristojah has long wanted to get rid of Mir Alum, but that the influence of the English always saved him. That at last Aristojah took advantage of the vanity and passions of young Kirkpatrick to make an attack upon the honour of the Mir which he could not but feel, and which he was obliged to resent. He thus deprived him of the support which had hitherto sustained him against all attacks. Mir Alum wrote to Lord Wellesley to complain of the treatment he had received from Kirkpatrick: the latter declared it was a foul calumny. . . . It was reported to the Nizam's court, and they reported that there was no foundation in it.

Noting that Mir Alum had been more concerned about his own position than about family scandal, the letter continues:

Mir Alum said nothing regarding the attack upon the honour of his family, but Akil ud Dowlah swore . . . that the whole story was true, that the woman slept at Kirkpatrick's house every night and that she is now with child. I know also from other quarters that he is married to her. . . . Mir Alum urged strongly the general impropriety and folly of Kirkpatrick's behaviour; he said that as a friend to the British nation he had thought it his duty to represent his conduct to the Governor General. . . . Among other things he told me that Kirkpatrick always appeared in a Mussulman's dress of the finest texture, excepting when he was obliged to receive officers of the detachment or upon certain great occasions when the etiquette of the Nizam's Durbar required that the English Resident should appear in the dress of an Englishman, and many other things equally ridiculous. . . . It will be impossible, in my opinion, to do anything for Mir Alum. The strong desire of Aristojah to get rid of him is the cause of his removal from the presence. Supposing the representations to Lord Wellesley and the proof of Kirkpatrick's ridiculous conduct should occasion his removal from Hyderabad, his successor could not insist upon the return of Mir Alum . . . unless indeed Aristojah were to sacrifice his friend Hashmat Jang and to swear that his interference was the cause of the Mir's temporary disgrace.

A son was born to James Achilles and Khair un Nissa on 4th March 1801, and James wrote to the Governor General explaining that he had 'hearkened to the voice of nature pleading eloquently in the engaging form of a helpless infant'. The scandal continued, however, and the letters—which took weeks to travel between Calcutta and Hyderabad—got longer and longer. A second child, a daughter, was born to Khair un Nissa on 9th April 1802, and the following month Lord Wellesley decided on a further step. He instructed John Malcolm, who had been Envoy to Persia and Kirkpatrick's assistant in Hyderabad four years earlier, and was now acting as a kind of travelling ambassador for the Governor General, to investigate the whole business again on the spot, and if necessary supersede Kirkpatrick.

When Malcolm reached Masulipatam on the way, however, he was met by the Captain of the Resident's cavalry, who assured him that even if Malcolm disproved the scandal and decided in Kirkpatrick's favour, the enquiry itself would be extremely damaging to British prestige. Malcolm agreed; he passed through Hyderabad to Poona without raising the question, and was able to satisfy Wellesley that it would be better to take no action.

The diplomatic branch of the Company's service in which the Residents served was the one with the highest status, and Wellesley picked the best of his staff to fill the posts and the most promising of the young Company Writers or soldiers to be trained for them. The other branches of the service—which would eventually become the famous Indian Civil Service—were the Judicial, which provided the senior judges, and the rank and file Executive, which provided the District Officers.

In 1800 James's brother, Edward's friend William, was appointed Resident at Poona to deal with the troublesome Peshwa, and Elphinstone that of Edward's assistant. Elphinstone was delighted, being eager to see new people and new places, but Edward, who greatly preferred the Judicial Branch, was reluctant.

As Elphinstone wrote in his diary:

Strachey says that he is unwilling to break into the quiet into which he is settled and he is afraid that he shall have less leisure at Poonah than here. He was unwilling to answer so soon and talked of seeing Kirkpatrick: I said he would do well to call on him to ask whether the business of the agency would take up much of his time, and if he should say it would employ the assistant constantly the offer ought to be rejected. Strachey said he would like to bargain that if he disliked the place he might return without it being taken amiss. I said that as the reason for sending us was that young civil servants might be fitted for the diplomatic line it could not be expected that we should be allowed to leave it without some good reason—that even should Lord Wellesley promise not to take our return amiss, his promise could not prevent his being displeased at the failure of his plan for educating young civilians.

Edward was clearly convinced, either by Elphinstone's sensible arguments or by further advice from William, for only three weeks later they all set out.

The route they took seems extraordinary now, but to sail to the west coast was considered too dangerous, as French ships would attack on sight, while the direct route overland was almost as risky. They therefore zig-zagged across almost the whole of India, taking nearly a year *en route*, going south from Calcutta along the coast to Madras, thence west to Mysore before turning northwards to Hyderabad, where they spent three months, before proceeding west again to Poona.

Both young men kept diaries, though Edward seems to have abandoned his before they arrived at Madras. They travelled in great state and strength, with a following of eight elephants, eleven camels, four horses and ten bullocks, not to mention the ponies and bullocks of the servants, of whom there were between 150 and 200, together with 20 sepoys, while they were joined later by what Elphinstone called 'A Mahratta condottiere of 30 to 40 men'.

All this was, of course, in honour of Kirkpatrick, but he was taken ill at the very outset, and went by sea as far as Madras instead.

The two young men, joined by an officer called Hamilton who was bound for Hyderabad to join James Achilles, had a most enjoyable journey. They had packed one elephant with a remarkable collection of books to read *en route*, including the history of the Bengal Mutiny by Edward's father, the Persian poets, Homer, Hesiod, Herodotus, Theocritus, Sappho, Plato, Machiavelli, Cowley, Horace Walpole, Bacon, Boswell and—surprisingly enough—Thomas Jefferson.

These they enjoyed, discussed and annotated in their journals as they passed on their way in their palanquins, camping among mango groves, startling the inland-born elephants with a first sight of the sea, hopefully believing tree-trunks were tigers and wandering between the jungle and the river, or playing the flute by the light of the moon.

Elphinstone was slow in learning Persian, and preferred Homer and Horace, but Edward inspired him with some of his own enthusiasm for the language and its poets. They were free to wander as they wished, passing the Juggernaut Temple at Puri (by which they were not impressed) and sightseeing in the Ghats, sometimes as much as 50 miles off-course.

When they reached the Godavery river they received a message from William Kirkpatrick in Madras telling them to come straight there by boat. They left the servants and tents, therefore, to be rejoined later, and hurried on. They found that not only was William no better, but that he had been forced to abandon the Poona project altogether and though still only in his forties was returning to England for good: the young men, however, were to continue. Elphinstone pushed on to rendezvous with the suite, while Edward spent about a month in Madras, where his cousin George, the Archdeacon's son, was then stationed. He was a year younger than Edward, still unreconciled to life in India, and said to be querulous and lonely.

It was now August 1801, and the next destination, after a reunion in Bangalore, was Seringapatam, to visit and obtain instructions from Colonel Arthur Wellesley. He received them most hospitably, and took them riding 'over very stony ground' noted Elphinstone, while Edward was called upon to prescribe for a sick child.

After this they were due at Hyderabad, to visit William's brother. Colonel Wellesley, hearing this, 'as usual rowed Hashmat Jang' no doubt for his 'idiotic' behaviour.

The friends seem to have been somewhat influenced by Wellesley's adverse opinion of James Achilles, for although they admitted that 'great and just credit' was given to him for the decisive steps he took to disband the French troops, they regarded the prospect of staying with him in the Residency with some disgust. 'Note from Hamilton', writes Elphinstone, 'asking in Major Kirkpatrick's name to live with him. Bore! Who would like to live with Hashmat Jang.' They did indeed find the diplomatic conversation at the Residency, about, for instance, the exclusion of the French from the court, extremely boring.

'Major Kirkpatrick is a goodlooking man', went on Elphinstone, 'he seems about 30 [actually he was 37 at this time and had recently been made a Major]. He wears mustachios, his hair is cropped very short, and his fingers are dyed with henna. In other respects he is dressed like an Englishman. He is very communicative, and very desirous to please; but he tells long stories about himself, makes all sorts of odd noises and practises all the affectations of which the face and eyes are capable. He offered me a horse, which I declined.'

James Achilles, for his part, reported a visit from 'Two superior young men, passing through Hyderabad on their way to Poona'.

He was certainly a very different kind of character from Strachey and Elphinstone. There is no mention in any of his letters of his ordering any books, or of any reading he had done, whereas the journals and letters of the other two are full of books they are reading, and of books ordered from England and what they thought of them. Kirkpatrick was a man of action, and a remarkably generous and affectionate one, pressing £1,000 a year on his brother William on his retirement, sending home frequent and valuable gifts for his nieces and presenting the children of his friends with boxes of toys.

Elphinstone does not mention Khair un Nissa, but Richard Strachey, Edward's brother, who also visited Hyderabad at one time, reported on his return, 'We never saw the lady, but we used to see Hashmat Jang crossing the Residency court and going to his zenana.'

Edward and Elphinstone accompanied James Achilles to a Durbar of the Nizam, and described the pomp of the occasion. 'James Achilles Kirkpatrick goes in great state. He has several elephants and a state palanquin, led horses, flags, long poles with tassels, etc, and is tended by two companies of infantry and a troop of cavalry.' They were received amicably by the Nizam, now an old and failing man, and also by Aristojah, the Wazir, and were surprised to find female sentries at the door, together with some 20 or 30 women dressed something like Madras sepoys. This was the Amazonian corps known as the Zuffer Puttan, who guarded the Nizam's harem of 600 wives. 'Major Kirkpatrick' said Elphinstone, 'behaved like a native and with great propriety'.

The two friends stayed three months in Hyderabad before completing their journey to Poona, by which time Colonel Close had been appointed Resident in William's place. After this they were attached for a time to Colonel Wellesley's staff and Elphinstone went to take part as interpreter in the battle of

Assaye, where he won more praise for his martial talents than for his interpreting. He later became Governor of Bombay, and would have gone on to be Governor General but for poor health. He was one of the best loved and most respected of British statesmen in India; even more than Cornwallis, Elphinstone was a man of outstanding integrity and goodness of heart.

Edward finally managed to get himself transferred from political to judicial work and served as a judge in a number of Indian courts. Before leaving Poona he was sent on a mission to the Mahrattas which was not wholly successful. However he received a letter of approval from Arthur Wellesley: '5.12.1804 Seringapatam. I am fully satisfied that you did everything in your power to bring your negotiations to a speedy and successful conclusion; and I am convinced that they failed from causes which were not foreseen when you were despatched on your mission and which you could not control. The result of your mission however, although not exactly what I could have wished, has been attended by many circumstances of public advantage . . . the public are indebted for them to your zeal, intelligence and ability.'

Edward never lost his interest in mathematics and wrote one book on *The History of Asian mathematics* and one on *The Algebra of the Hindoos*.

In 1808 when he was 34, he married the 18-year-old Julia, youngest and prettiest of the four daughters of William Kirkpatrick, who had come out to Calcutta to visit her sister Barbara Buller wife of Charles Buller, MP; three years later they returned permanently to England.

At the time when Edward and Elphinstone stayed in Hyderabad, the Residency was based in a group of bungalows forming part of one of the summer palaces of the Wazir, but James Achilles was far from satisfied with this accommodation, both on his own account and on that of the Company, and determined to build himself a more worthy mansion. His wife brought him considerable riches and his official funds were large. He knew, too, that he could rely on the fabulously wealthy Nizam to make up anything needed.

The first requirement was a site, and he fixed on a property of some 60 acres across the river Musi on the edge of the city. He employed a lieutenant of the Madras engineers, Samuel Russell, as an architect, and they drew up a plan to show the Nizam. To Kirkpatrick's disappointment the Nizam rejected this with great force, but the Wazir explained privately that he was not used to maps, and the plan had been drawn on so large a scale that he thought the site must cover most of his dominions. So James Achilles had another plan made, no larger than a postcard, whereupon the Nizam agreed with delight, and leased him the land for one rupee a year.

The first stage was to prepare a zenana for Khair un Nissa, with temporary accommodation for James Achilles himself. This was to the south east of the main building, with its own gate, and was a pavilion called the Rang Mahal, the Palace of Colours, from the paintings of birds, flowers and beasts with which it was decorated. Nearby a private walled garden with fountains was also constructed for Khair un Nissa, and in it he had built for her a small model of the projected mansion. This garden is still known as the Begum's garden, and the model still exists, though it is unfortunately much decayed.*

Work was started on the new Residency in 1803; it was finished in 1808 and was, apart from Calcutta and later New Delhi, the grandest of all the British palaces in India. To the north it had a classical pilastered front, with a broad flight of steps leading up to it, while the south entrance, called the Imperial Gate, was flanked by elephant stables and cavalry lines and looked out on to a small lake. Inside the palace was a huge Durbar Hall, with parquet flooring, and a grand staircase, while from the ceiling hung an enormous chandelier purchased by the Company from the ever penurious Prince of Wales. Kirkpatrick, like Clive, was fond of collecting animals, and the park was full of deer, Abyssinian goats, elk and all manner of birds. A telescope was ordered for the terrace and thousands of Chinese lanterns to light up the house and grounds when entertainments were to be given.

James Achilles himself, however, did not live to see his palace finished. He was a most loving father to his son and daughter,

* The Residency is now a college for girls in the University of Hyderabad.

referring to them as his 'dear little ones' in letters, and in 1805, with their mother's reluctant consent, they were sent to England—as so many English children were, over the years—to be brought up there in the home of their grandfather and their uncle William. To comfort her a picture of the two was painted by George Chinnery, an English artist well known for his Indian portraits.

The children, now four and three, were to take the long sea journey in the care of the wife of the English surgeon in Hyderabad, with an English nurse and an Indian manservant. They left Madras on 9th September 1805.

Cornwallis had again been appointed Governor General on Wellesley's recall, charged with extravagance and expansionist campaigns, and as soon as he arrived he summoned James Achilles (now a Lieutenant Colonel) together with other Residents, to brief him on their respective areas and problems and on Wellesley's policy in general.

James Achilles set sail at once from Madras, but was taken ill on the journey with an acute but unidentified fever. In Calcutta he stayed at the house of his niece, Barbara Buller, and there he died on 15th October aged 41, less than a month after the children had left.

His Will, made six months before his death, is a moving document. In it he directed that his debts be paid, his 'natural son Sahib Alum, born at Hyderabad of a Mussulman Lady of Birth and Distinction' and his 'natural daughter, born also at Hyderabad of the same amiable and distinguished Mussulman lady, and commonly called Saheb Begum' should each receive £12,000. He left each of his four 'beloved nieces' whom he stated that he would have adopted had he had no children of his own, £3,000. Many other bequests were listed; to William 'the best of brothers', to cousins, colleagues and staff, and to two natural daughters of his father (who appears to have had several illegitimate children) whom he feared might be indigent, and who were to get £1,000 each. 'The poor unhappy women to whom I allude will I trust, if still in existence, be found out and recognised by the foregoing description.'

As to his wife, who must have brought him much of his

considerable wealth, he said: 'The excellent and respectable Mother of my two natural children, who is named Khair un Nissa Begum, being amply provided for by Jagirs and other possessions both hereditary and acquired, independent of her personal property and jewels which cannot amount to less than half a lakh of rupees, I have not thought it necessary to provide particularly for her. By way of proof, however, of my unbounded love and affection towards her and as a token of my Esteem and Remembrance' he left her too £12,000.

By describing his children as 'natural', making them Wards in Chancery and expressing a 'wish, intention and most positive and urgent injunction' to have them christened as soon as they arrived in England', he made it clear that whatever his actions may have been at the time of his wedding to Khair un Nissa, he did not believe it to be a legal wedding from the English point of view.

The day before he died he added a thoughtful codicil, directing that the bequests to his nieces were to be paid on marriage and not necessarily to await their 21st birthdays.

There is no record of what befell the unfortunate Khair un Nissa. Some say she took ship to rejoin her children and went down in a typhoon off Ceylon; some say she went to Calcutta to live with the Bullers, and some that she returned to Hyderabad from Madras to find that all her possessions had been removed from the Rang Mahal and that she had been supplanted by a cousin called Lutf un Nissa, who had contracted an alliance with Henry Russell, erstwhile assistant to Kirkpatrick and later Resident himself. Others say, on the other hand, that Henry Russell befriended her and advised her to move to Masulipatam. There is no evidence for any of these stories, though it appears that she was paid an allowance (presumably the Jagir referred to in the Will) for several years. It is most likely that she returned to her mother's household and there died not long after. Some of the letters later written by her mother to her children, illuminated for her by a Persian scribe, still survive, but there are none from Khair un Nissa herself.

LONDON AND THOMAS CARLYLE

Kitty Kirkpatrick

(1808–78)

When they first returned from India, after their marriage in 1808, Edward and his young wife Julia lived at Sutton Court, which his brother Henry, who preferred to live at Rook's Nest, had loaned them.

They stayed there for some years, and Edward took an intelligent interest in farming. Indeed at one stage he bought a farm of his own. 'My last accounts from home,' wrote his brother Richard from Gwalior to his friend John Adam, political Secretary to the Governor General, 'say that Ned has bought a farm near Chippenham in an ugly country. He was living at my brother Henry's house in Somersetshire and had been a good deal in Bath with the Bullers. . . . I don't hear whether he proposes moving to his own Domain or not, but if he does he must think of putting up in a Barn or of encamping, for I understand the Estate has no home upon it.'

Clearly no house was built, and no more is heard of the Chippenham property. Meanwhile Edward acted as Justice of the Peace in the Sutton Court area. He had had, of course, considerable judicial experience in India, and when faced with poachers and other Somersetshire miscreants he often found himself taking notes in Persian, as he had been in the habit of doing with Indian dacoits.

In 1819 there was a reorganization of what was called the 'Examiner's office' of the East India Company in Leadenhall Street, and three new senior men were taken on to assess incoming despatches and to draft and write replies. The three men appointed were Edward Strachey, on the judicial side, Thomas Love Peacock, author of *Headlong Hall* and *Nightmare Abbey*, on the Public Works side, and James Mill (father of John Stuart Mill) who had recently written a history of India, to deal with financial matters.

These three worked together in one room, and Edward and Peacock soon became close friends. Both of them, however, had reservations about the somewhat cold and bigoted Mill, and the Strachey family particularly disliked him because they believed that he had conspired to get himself promoted above Edward.

Peacock was a man of warmth and humour, fond of good living, tolerant and indulgent. Mill, on the other hand, was grim and opinionated, argued savagely in defence of his views and followed his own philosophy that man's only motivation in life was self-interest. When a friend asked Peacock what Mill was like and wondered: 'Would he hate what I hate and like what I like?' Peacock replied: 'He will hate what you hate *and* hate everything you like.'

Being himself of a similarly malignant character, Mill, in his history of India, had accepted the biased attacks on Warren Hastings made by Philip Francis and supported by Burke. It was this bias which inspired Macaulay, in his turn, to write with such eloquent and unsupported venom of Clive and Hastings, and it was not until a generation later that the writings of Edward's son John and of James Fitzjames Stephen finally exonerated and reinstated Hastings.

When he started his new work Edward moved with his family to London, and took a house in Fitzroy Square and a summer home called Goodenough House on Shooter's Hill, near Woolwich. He was lyrical about this place, and wrote to his old friend, Mountstuart Elphinstone, from the office:

> I have got a very nice place on Shooter's Hill 8 miles from this part of town. There in the summer I enjoy the fine air, the cool shade of the trees, the grand and splendid view of the Thames with London and its spires—St Pauls and Westminster Abbey—showing obscurely in the distance through its mellowing mass of smoke and fog—the hills at its back stretching out parallel to the line of the Thames . . . a highly cultivated rich green country with hamlets, villages and spires. . . . The river I see for 2 miles below me . . . till at last it is lost in a

vast forest of masts just visible in the palpable obscure of
London. . . . I am generally in my garden about six in the
morning. There I saunter, interesting myself about the business of that department for an hour or two. Then I walk or go
in my gig 3 miles to Blackheath, thence in a stage coach to
town.

He worked, he said, from ten to four, and finished by saying:
'You will wonder, as do others, at my liking my occupation
here—but I do like it.'

Edward had always loved the river, and claimed that as early as
1793, before he went to India, he had seen a little model steamship
paddling to and fro near Blackfriars, with a steam funnel, paddle
wheels and 'other outfits'. Captains of Indiamen would often call
at Leadenhall Street with news on their way upriver. They still
used St Helena as a port of call, and in that way Edward first learnt
of the death of Napoleon an hour or two, as he used to boast,
before the Government.

Edward's sister-in-law, Barbara Buller, had now returned to
England, and in 1824 had appointed the young Thomas Carlyle,
who had just arrived in London, as tutor to her young sons,
Charles and Arthur. Through this connection Carlyle got to
know the Stracheys and to visit Shooter's Hill, and became a
lifelong friend of the family, especially of Julia. As he reported,
they treated him 'as a near relation, not a wandering stranger'.

Carlyle, too, was enthusiastic about Goodenough House. He
called it 'A modestly excellent house' and the garden 'an
umbrageous little park with roses'.

He described Edward to his brother as 'a little bustling, logic-
chopping good-hearted, frank fellow' and painted a characteristic
portrait of him in his *Reminiscences*.

Edward Strachey was a genially abrupt man; 'Utilitarian' and
Democrat in creed, yet beyond all things he loved Chaucer and
kept reading him. A man rather tacit than discursive; but
willing to speak and doing it well in a fine tinkling mellow-
toned voice, in an ingenious aphoristic way—had withal a
pretty vein of quiz which he seldom indulged in; a man sharply

impatient of pretence, of sham and untruth in all forms—
especially contemptuous of 'quality' pretensions and affectations, which he scattered grinningly to the winds . . . scorned
cheerfully 'the general humbug of the world' and honestly
strove to do his own bit of duty, spiced by Chaucer and what
else of inward harmony or condiment he had. Of religion in
articulate shape he had none; but much respected his Wife's,
whom, and whose truthfulness in all things he tenderly
esteemed and loved. A man of many qualities: comfortable to
be near.

Julia, on the other hand, was deeply religious and was attracted
to the Evangelical 'Clapham Sect', whose pious members, it was
said, would ask each other at intervals 'Shall we engage?' and
drop to their knees. Above all she was a follower of the strange,
credulous Scottish preacher Edward Irving. Irving, a handsome
man—but for a pronounced squint—had a chapel first in Hatton
Garden and later in Regent Street, where he would preach to a
congregation of a thousand for three hours on end. He believed in
the gift of tongues and in miraculous cures, though he was no
quack himself but was modest about his own lack of supernatural
gifts.

Carlyle had been his friend in Scotland in the early days, and
though he had no high opinion of Irving's intellect and often
found him comical, was genuinely fond of the preacher and called
him 'The Orator'.

Irving was the first man to whom Carlyle turned on his arrival
in London. The preacher had recently married and moved into a
new house, where he invited Carlyle to dine. On Carlyle's arrival
he found that two wealthy and charitable ladies had furnished his
host's house at their own expense as a surprise. The two ladies
were Julia Strachey and her cousin, Kitty Kirkpatrick, daughter
of James Achilles Kirkpatrick and Khair un Nissa.

The two Kirkpatrick children, on their arrival in England early
in 1806, had been taken to live first with their grandfather at his
home Hollydale, near Bromley in Kent, and on his death with
their cousin, Julia's sister Clementina, wife of Admiral Lord
Louis.

Their mother had been bitterly unhappy at the separation and had insisted, before they left, on endowing them both handsomely, so they were brought up as well-to-do English children. Following their father's wishes they were both christened on arrival; the boy, originally known as Shah Jehan, Mir Goolaum Ali, or Sahib Alum, in India, became William George, called after his two uncles, and the daughter, Nur un Nissa, Chootee Angrezi Begum, became Katherine Aurora, known as Kitty, after her Munro grandmother and great-aunt.

At first they pined for their parents and longed to return from cold England to the warmth of Hyderabad, but as they grew up they became more reconciled. William, who was given to dwelling on Wordsworth's poetry and the metaphysics of Coleridge, had always been considered vague and dreamy—as a result, his friends claimed, of falling into a copper of boiling water in childhood. This accident may have led to his early death in 1828, but did not prevent his marrying and begetting three daughters first.

His sister Kitty grew up to be merry, sensible and attractive. Carlyle wrote of her:

She had one of the prettiest smiles, a visible sense of humour, the slight merry curl of her upper lip *right side* of it only, the carriage of her head and eyes on such occasions, the quiet little things she said in that kind and her low-toned hearty laugh, were noticeable . . . of developed intellect she had not much, though not wanting in discernment. Amiable, affectionate, graceful, might be called attractive (not *slim* enough for the title 'pretty' not tall enough for 'beautiful') had something low-voiced, languidly harmonious, placid, sensuous, loved perfume etc, a half-*Begum* in short, interesting specimen of the semi-Oriental Englishwoman.

Both her cousin Julia, who was eleven years older than she, and Edward were very fond of her and she spent much of her time staying with the Stracheys at Shooter's Hill. Kitty had a particular respect for Edward, and in old age still remembered that in doubtful cases she had always, in her thoughts, referred every issue of right and wrong to what his judgement would have been.

On one occasion Kitty copied out a poem by Shelley for Edward, and elicited a very typical response. He told her that he did not admire it, and had taken it to Peacock, who did not admire it either, and said it was without truth to nature. Edward added: 'I don't see why common sense should be dispensed with in verse any more than in prose.' Unfortunately the identity of the poem can no longer be established.

Although he had already told Julia of his attachment to Jane Welsh, Carlyle clearly fell a little in love with Kitty Kirkpatrick, too. Soon after he got to know her he wrote to Jane:

> This Kitty is a singular and very pleasing creature; a little blackeyed, auburn-haired brunette, full of kindliness and humour, and who never, I believe, was angry at any creature for a moment in her life. Tho' twenty one and not unbeautiful, and sole mistress of herself and fifty thousand pounds, she is meek and modest as a Quakeress; with a demure eye she surveys the extravagances of the Orator laughing at him in secret, yet loving him as a good man. . . . Good Kitty, would you or I were half as happy as this girl.

Jane, predictably enough, was jealous. 'I congratulate you on your present situation. With such a picture of domestic felicity before your eyes, and this "singular and very pleasing creature" to charm away the blue-devils, you can hardly fail to be as happy as the day is long. Miss Kitty Kirkpatrick—Lord what an ugly name! Oh pretty, dear and delightful Kitty! I am not a bit jealous of her, not I indeed—Hindoo princess though she be! Only you may as well never let me hear you mention her name again!'

That autumn of 1824 Julia Strachey arranged a seaside holiday in Dover for herself and Kitty, to be joined later by Edward, while Carlyle was staying with the Irvings who had a house there. Irving and his wife Isabella had a new baby, and Carlyle and Kitty derived much amusement from the father's doting ways. He would say solemnly to Isabella: 'I would wash him, I think, in *warm* water tonight.' 'Kitty Kirkpatrick smiles

covertly,' said Carlyle, 'and I laugh aloud at the earnest devoted-
ness of the good Orator to this weighty affair.'

They would stroll in the lanes in the afternoons and in the
evenings Irving would read aloud—somewhat pompously, Kitty
and Thomas agreed. Edward, when he arrived, was even less in
sympathy with the preacher, and Julia finally decided that they
were all too frivolous to allow her to have serious uninterrupted
sessions with Irving, so she persuaded the other three to set off on
a jaunt to Paris in a hired carriage.

As they drove through France they took it in turns to sit outside
and enjoy the scenery. None of them spoke French at all well.
Edward with an entertaining dose of vanity had claimed that he
spoke it like a native, but it turned out that his mastery of the
language was virtually non-existent and diminished every day. In
Beauvais he could be heard scolding the waiters: 'C'est bien
imposants, c'est une—une rascalité, vous dis'je; vous avez chargé
deux fois trop.' And at each Post he shrieked: 'Où est les
chevaux?' As Carlyle reported: 'When a man asked him for
"quelquechose à boire, je vous ai conduit très bien," Strachey
answered, without looking at him: "Nong! Vous avez drivé
devilish slow."'

When they reached Paris he gave up the battle altogether, and,
as Carlyle said: 'would speak nothing but English, which, aided
by his vivid looks and gestures he found, in shops and the like, to
answer much better.' There were further linguistic problems,
however, when they went to call on M. de Chezy, Professor of
Sanskrit at the Collège de France, with whom Edward and his
brother had corresponded in Persian from India. Edward
embarked at once on a discourse in Persian, delighted to be able to
speak the beloved language again, but de Chezy's Persian was as
French as Edward's French was English, and after a frustrating
twenty minutes they departed.

Carlyle left London in the following year, and married his Jane
a year after that, though he returned to London to live in 1834. He
still kept in touch with the Stracheys and Bullers, and often
thought—and even occasionally dreamed—of Kitty Kirkpatrick.

In 1828 Charles Buller, his old pupil, had left Cambridge and
was preparing for a political career. Julia Strachey asked Carlyle

to help her cure Charles of the irreligious tendencies he was beginning to show, and Carlyle did his best, but without much result. Charles remained friendly, however, and in August 1828 he sent Carlyle news of the various family troubles. 'Mrs Strachey', he wrote, 'has just had the misfortune of—a tenth child. We have some expectations of seeing Miss Kirkpatrick soon, but she is in great trouble. Her brother William, perhaps you already know, died in May after a lingering and painful illness. His poor young wife has gone mad, and Kitty, after all this, has been involved in a very wearisome dispute with Mrs Kirkpatrick's sister respecting the care of her brother's children.'

A year later Kitty married Captain James Winsloe Phillipps of the Seventh Hussars, and went to live in Torquay. She had three daughters and one son, John James, later known as 'Uncle Beau' who married Charlotte Strachey, daughter of the handsome Richard Strachey who had been on the expedition to Persia.

Soon after this Carlyle wrote his curious fable, *Sartor Resartus*—a work perhaps more widely read and appreciated in its own day than it is now. It concerned partly the philosophy of clothes and partly the adventures of Professor Teufelsdröckh with the high class Zahldarm family and his love for the beautiful Blumine, who after making the Professor immortal—he declared—with a single kiss, married another. It was assumed that the book was a *roman à clef*, with Teufelsdröckh a self-portrait, and there was much controversy, then and later, over the identity of the heroine, Blumine.

Some scholars asserted that she was Carlyle's first love, Margaret Gordon, and some that she was partly Jane Welsh, partly Kitty and partly imaginary. The Strachey family, however, were never in any doubt, from the nature of the detailed descriptions of places and people, that Blumine was Kitty, and that other members of their family, together with Irving—the Orator—were also represented. Kitty would not commit herself, though she was once heard to take Carlyle laughingly to task about Blumine's kiss. 'You know you were never made immortal in that manner,' she said. She lived to be 87, and in old age she was asked outright if she was really Blumine. She kept her secret to the last and said: 'What does it matter? It all happened a long time ago.'

As they grew up the Kirkpatrick children had lost touch with India, and their family there, but after she was married, Kitty met by chance, in Exmouth, a Mrs Malcolm, wife of Captain Duncan Malcolm who had just been appointed Resident at Hyderabad, who offered to try to make contact for her.

From what Malcolm wrote to Kitty it appears likely that after Khair un Nissa's death the Nizam's government deliberately cut off all correspondence between her mother and England. They also appear to have sequestered her estate, though a pension was paid her, albeit irregularly.

Malcolm visited the old lady, Sherf un Nissa Begum, and believed that, although he was not permitted to interfere on her behalf, the fact that he had taken an interest would stimulate more regular payments.

The old lady complained bitterly about having been kept for many years without information about the children, and begged Kitty to send her a pair of European spectacles—'a pair adapted for an old lady of 80 with tolerable eyesight'.

Kitty was anxious to find proof that her parents were truly married, but as the marriage contract could not be found, all the witnesses were dead and the new Nizam clearly unhelpful, this was not forthcoming, though Sherf un Nissa sent Kitty a detailed description of the ceremony.

Finally Kitty wrote to her grandmother:

I often think of you and remember you and my dear mother. I often dream that I am with you in India and that I see you both in the room you used to sit in. No day of my life has ever passed without my thinking of my dear mother. I can remember the veranda and the place where the tailors worked and a place on the house top where my mother used to let me sit down and slide. When I dream of my mother I am in such joy to have found her again that I awake or else I am pained in finding that she cannot understand the English I speak. . . . I can well recollect her cries when we left her and I can now see the place in which she sat when we parted, and her tearing her long hair—what worlds would I give to possess one lock of that beautiful and much loved hair.

'It is after 35 years', she went on, 'I am able for the first time to hear that you think of me and love me and have perhaps wondered why I did not write to you and that you have thought me cold and insensible to such near dear ties. I thank God that He has opened for me a way of making the feelings of my heart known to you.'

Sherf un Nissa, in a letter written—or rather illuminated—for her by a Persian scribe and translated by Malcolm, answered: 'The letter written to me by my child is pressed by me sometimes to my head and sometimes to my eyes. It is written in it that my child has married a nephew of Sir John Kennaway [a previous resident at Hyderabad]. The receipt of this news, replete with gladness, has added joy upon joy to me.'

And when Kitty told her that her brother William's eldest daughter, now nineteen, was to marry a doctor who was going to India, she wrote back: 'My heart cannot contain the joy it feels in learning that the daughter of Sahib Alum is about to visit Hindostan with her husband, and I will, without fail, cherish the child as the apple of my eye.'

Edward Strachey died suddenly at Shooter's Hill in January 1832. Among many friends from his Indian days the closest was still Mountstuart Elphinstone, who would often come to stay with him at Goodenough House and have enjoyable discussions on past adventures and recent books. 'I heard the sad account of the death of Strachey,' he commented when he heard the news, 'to whose early advice and friendship I owe so much, and on whose continued friendship I depended for a great portion of my future life.'

Julia moved to Clifton, near Bristol; she lived on for fourteen years there, and then died of a fever on a visit to Italy, and was buried in Florence. She had remained intellectually active, learning Greek and Hebrew to read the Bible, and struggling also with German. Her friendship with Carlyle was unbroken: he wrote frequently and came to visit her in Clifton from time to time. He had a real and admiring affection for her and retained it to the end of his life, respecting, as her husband had done, her 'religious nature and truthful character', and calling her 'a singular pearl of a woman'. Six months after her death he was still missing her, and wrote to her son Edward: 'The melancholy message which reached me last winter has not, even yet, produced its whole effect on me. New days and events turn up ever new remembrances, sad and sacred. . . . Surely the remembrance of your noble mother will never leave me while I live in this world.'

He did not forget Kitty, either, and asked after her frequently, while she would sometimes visit him in Cheyne Row, though her welcome from Jane was always a frosty one.

The family friendship was carried over to the next generation, to Julia's six sons, four of whom went to India. Carlyle, said George, the youngest son, greatly approved of the British connection with India, and 'Members of the junior generation of our family returning from Tibet or from Rajpootana or Almira, or from the battlefields of Aliwal and Sobraon, were thus doubly welcome in Cheyne Row.' The family also remained friendly with Kitty, who was related to them once again by marriage, and would see her whenever possible.

In 1877 Richard, the third son, visited the aged Carlyle and reported him as being 'in complete possession of his faculties, in good spirits and full of his usual fun'. He would sit on the floor, smoking his long clay pipe and occasionally patting his cat, Tib. This was the last they saw of him.

THE SENIOR LINE

Edward Strachey and his sons

(1812–1927)

Edward Strachey and Julia Kirkpatrick had twelve children in all; six sons, all of whom survived to old age, and six daughters, five of whom died young. The only girl to survive, Jane, married a carpet manufacturer in Bristol, called Hare.

The eldest of the six sons, born in 1812 at Sutton Court, was also called Edward. Like his father, both grandfathers, two great-uncles and two uncles, he fully expected to go to India, and was sent to Haileybury, the school founded by the East India Company to train its future employees and teach them the languages they would need.

Sir Edward Strachey (1812–1901) as a child, with a sister Charlotte
who died young

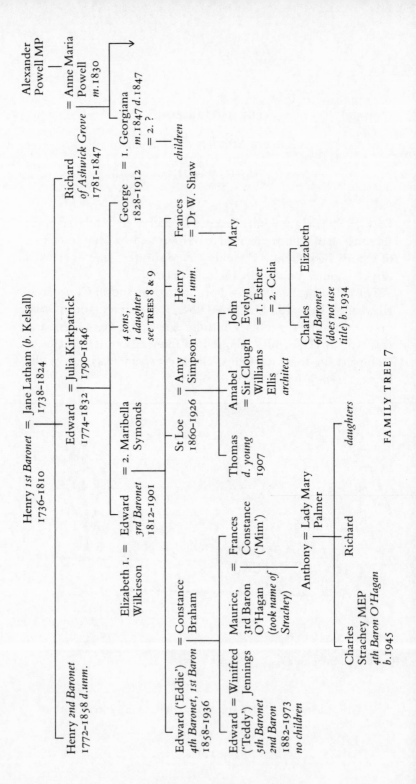

FAMILY TREE 7

Just before he was due to sail, however, he was attacked by a severe infection of the knee, which reduced him to crutches and an invalid chair for twenty years and ruined his chances of going to India.

In the 1850s he twice spent the winter in Naples—'for his health', though at that time it was notoriously corrupt and unhealthy. In fact, however, his health did seem to have benefited, for after 'taking the waters' at Ischia he was able to walk without crutches, though his knee was always stiff and he remained lame and unable to ride.

Unlike his brothers, who were all sceptics in the Strachey tradition, he took after his mother in being, and remaining, deeply religious, though he disliked her Evangelical way of—as he called it—'living in one's spiritual shirtsleeves'. He was a convinced and reticent Anglican, always tolerant of the beliefs of others, even if he did not find them congenial.

In his twenties he read and was much impressed by the writings of F. D. Maurice. John Sterling, a good friend of Carlyle's who lived in Clifton, and whom Carlyle had introduced to Edward's mother, was at Cambridge with Maurice, and while there they had together founded the Apostles' Society, later to include so many writers and philosophers among its members.

Maurice took orders, but he made a rather disturbing clergyman, a good preacher and writer, but very politically minded, a Christian Socialist and not always orthodox in his theology. Edward, however, approved wholeheartedly of Maurice's views, and particularly of an essay called 'Subscription no Travesty', one of his less unconventional works, in which he put forward eloquent arguments urging that the clergy should continue to be required to subscribe to the ambiguous Thirty-nine Articles.

Sterling told Edward that Maurice, who was then Chaplain to Guy's Hospital, wanted a pupil to read with him for Oxford or Cambridge. Though he did not intend to go to a University, Edward got in touch with Maurice, they made immediate friends, and Edward went to live and study with him for six months, a period which had a lasting effect on his thought.

In 1844 he married Elizabeth Wilkieson, daughter of a clergy-man; it was a very happy, though childless marriage, and in his old age he remembered her as 'a perfect woman'. Eleven years later she died, and he soon decided to marry again. He set his heart on his cousin Georgiana, daughter of his uncle Richard Strachey of Ashwick, and was about to propose to her when his youngest brother George got there first. Edward then informed George that this was unsuitable, which caused a good deal of friction, though the brothers were ultimately reconciled. Georgiana duly married George, and Edward proposed to Mary Isabella, always known as Maribella, daughter of Dr John Addington Symonds and sister of the prolific writer, the younger John Addington Symonds. She was very young—only nine-teen—and was said by Edward's brothers to be 'not pretty but amiable and very fat'.

Edward had been a good friend of the Doctor's and a frequent visitor to his house for many years. At nineteen Maribella liked older men, and fell much in love with her lame, middle-aged suitor. They were married in Clifton parish church, and the Doctor was so overcome by emotion that he spent the whole afternoon in the Strachey drawing-room at Clifton Hill House, weeping.

This marriage too was a great success, though Maribella, like so many Victorian wives, took to her bed as an invalid as she got older. They had four children, three sons and one daughter, Frances.

In 1858 Edward's uncle, the second Sir Henry, died, and in accordance with his Will his coffin was carried in old-fashioned style on men's shoulders all the four or five miles from Sutton Court to Chew Magna parish church. Edward inherited the title and Sutton Court, which he immediately set to work to improve. It was still a happy jumble of medieval, Elizabethan and later architecture, surrounded by its crenellated walls and avenues of limes and elms, but it had been allowed to deteriorate sadly in Sir Henry's day.

None of the Stracheys had ever resembled the typical fictional country squire, following the hounds, drinking too much port, running up gambling debts, brutally enforcing the game laws and enclosing tenants' land. Nor had they ever been rich or grand. Even the eldest sons had always had to work, and while they had never been actually poor, since the disastrous days of Hodges Strachey and the £12,000 mortgage, neither did they live at all luxuriously.

Sir Edward was a true Victorian paternalist, and took a warm personal interest in his tenants. He served as a Justice of the Peace, Poor Law Guardian, deputy Lieutenant and High Sheriff of Somerset. Tenants, police and people on magistrate's business came to consult him at his house, as he was too lame to do much visiting himself, and he became known as—if anything—too concerned to defend the underdog. Among other gestures he had (like many other religious men) given up sugar as a very young man, in protest against slavery in the West Indies, and did not again take it until the slaves were freed.

He still had to deal with the occasional case of witchcraft, charges made by one old lady against another of nailing down her footprints or growing deadly nightshade with intent to poison. These he dealt with patiently, but was fiery against oppression and cruelty, particularly to children.

His main interest, however, was in books. He had a largish library and wrote frequently and well for the more serious periodicals on literary and historical subjects. He could read French, Italian, Greek and Latin, and like his mother learnt Hebrew for his Biblical and theological studies. Like his father and maternal grandfather, William Kirkpatrick, however, his great love was for Persian poetry, which he read constantly and of which he tried to make his own translations.

The list of the books and articles he wrote is a very long one—there were 99 articles in the Spectator alone—and the scope was equally wide, ranging from *Shakespeare's Ghosts* to *Jewish history and politics at the time of Sennacherib*, and from *Holy Matrimony and the Church* to *Nonsense as a Fine Art*, including, towards the end of his life, a moving essay on *Old Age*.

Together with his small stature and dark eyes he had also inherited the family passion for cats. He was painted by his son Henry with his favourite cat, Jim, who was believed to be descended in the direct line from King George, the famous cat in the first Sir Henry's tapestry picture, and he used often to quote the Persian poet who wrote: 'The Almighty created cats so that mankind might have the felicity of caressing the tiger.'

His eldest son, Edward, married the niece of a near neighbour, Frances Lady Waldegrave, who was a romantic figure, married four times, and one of the great society and political hostesses of the period. She was also one of the principal patronesses of Edward Lear, author of the *Books of Nonsense*, and through this Sir Edward came to be a close friend of that strange and lonely man—another great cat-lover.

Lear used often to visit Sutton Court, and attended the wedding of the younger Edward at Cannes, near his own villa at San Remo. The whole family delighted in Lear's nonsense songs and pictures and Sir Edward wrote a preface for one of his books while the younger Edward's wife edited the books and letters and did much to make his name known. His letters were very typical and much treasured by the recipients. In December 1882, for instance, he wrote to Lady Strachey: 'I do not really believe you have any flowers—leastways roses. I feel sure you only see the refraction of those we have here—by some parallaxical effect of atmosphere which Sir Edward may explain, but I cannot, not understanding Astronomy, only Gastronomy. Anyhow we haven't had any frost here, and there are still—happily—some mosquitoes living, which, as it is warmer here than with you, is Gnatural.'

He would illustrate his letters to the children, as Henry Strachey described after a visit he paid to Lear's villa in the same year. 'On the last evening after dinner he wrote a letter for me to take back to my father, sending him the then unpublished conclusion to Mr and Mrs Discobbolus; and when this was done he took from a place in his bureau a number of carefully cut-out backs of old envelopes, and on these he drew, to send to my sister, then eight years old, the delightful series . . . of heraldic pictures of his cat. After he had done seven he said it was a great shame to caricature Foss, and laid aside his pen.'

This was Lear's second villa; the first had been made intolerable when a large hotel was built immediately in front of it, so he had a new one built overlooking the sea, exactly like the first. 'This, Mr

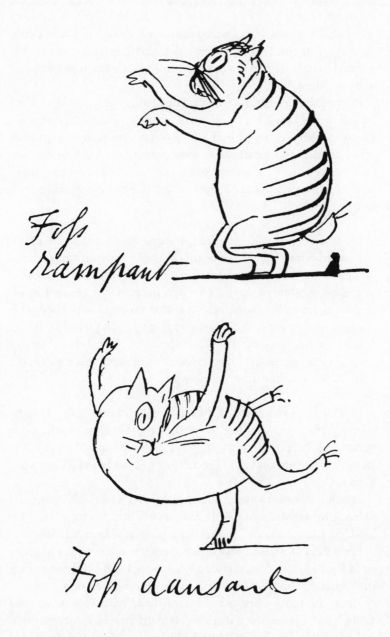

Foss
rampant

Foss dansant

Two heraldic blazons of Foss the Cat, by Edward Lear

Lear explained to me', said Henry, 'was necessary or else Foss, his cat, might not approve of the new villa.' In the afternoons, Henry went on, Lear usually answered the door himself, so that he could send away people that he did not like, particularly Germans. 'He seemed to have a great horror and fear that a German might be let in by accident.'

In appearance Sir Edward was small and slight, and in old age he was nearly blind. Poor sight was a family failing, and one of his brothers went entirely blind and another very nearly so in later life. His family was extremely fond of him, and his daughter-in-law, Amy, wife of his second son, St Loe, described his simplicity and sweetness of character, and wrote of her first meeting with him.

> He was very small, very frail, leaning on a stick, with a little pointed white Van Dyke beard, but with the most marvellous regard that I have ever seen. I have met two saints in my life, and he was one of them. Through his eyes one seemed to see shining his selfless soul, which at that moment was filled with eager love to welcome a new daughter . . . as I write I have an echo in my ears of his voice speaking with little gasps of eagerness, as if the tongue could not keep pace with the lightning quickness of the thought.

Sir Edward's eldest son, Edward, was known as Eddie. He was born in 1858 and gratified his father by taking to politics. He became a Liberal M.P. in 1892, was a Junior Whip and was made a Baron by Asquith in 1911. From 1912 to 1915 he was Paymaster General.

He did not, however, share his father's and his brother's literary or artistic tastes. He was a tall, handsome man with handlebar moustaches, and his main interest was in agriculture.

His wife, Constance, was vague about her appearance and given to Malapropisms. She was also a convinced anti-feminist during the agitation for Votes for Women, at the beginning of the century. In 1901 when Sir Edward died, both Constance and Eddie's aunt, Janie, the wife of Sir Richard Strachey, were known as Lady Strachey. Sir Richard's wife was a fierce and dedicated

Above left: Edward Strachey (1774–1832). Artist unknown
Above right: Julia Kirkpatrick Strachey (1790–1846). Artist unknown
Below left: Kitty Kirkpatrick (1802–89). From a miniature
Below right: Thomas Carlyle as a young man

John St Loe Strachey (1860–1926)

Sir Edward Strachey (1812–1901)
and his cat Jim, by his son,
Henry Strachey

Sir John Strachey (1824–1907)

Suffrage worker and the confusion in their names, which was always occurring, was exceedingly bitter to Constance. In 1911, however, Eddie was made a Baron. In those days only Law Lords could retain their family names as their titles, but Eddie wanted to continue to be known as Strachey, and so compromised by spelling the title Strachie, although there was no history of such a spelling in the past. Thus the two ladies, to Constance's great relief, ceased to be credited with views they loathed.

Eddie and Constance had two children, another Edward, known as Teddy, who became the second and last Lord Strachie, and a daughter, Frances known as 'Mim'.

Teddy was outstandingly handsome, and family tradition had it that he had been known as 'Venus' when in the Grenadier Guards. He married very late in life and had no children, and as the peerage, unlike the Baronetcy, was granted only in the direct male line, it died with him.

The youngest of Sir Edward's three sons, Henry, never married. He was a painter and musician, and lived in a house on the edge of the Sutton Court property, writing numerous articles on art and music for *The Spectator* and other similar periodicals, and painting somewhat pre-Raphaelite pictures, including bold wall-paintings for the local church. He was red-haired, a kindly modest man, one of the early Commissioners of the Boy Scout movement.

Sir Edward's second son, born in 1860, was called John St Loe, after the family who built Sutton Court. He became a journalist, owner-editor of *The Spectator* and a pillar of the Liberal Establishment of his day.

As a child he had had the normal youthful impatience with the older generation and refused, when his father offered to take him to call on Carlyle, though he later regretted this. He was educated for the most part at home by his father, and acquired a taste for mathematics and an almost inordinate love of poetry, of which he knew an enormous amount by heart. He had, however, little Latin or Greek, so when he came to be 18 and was due to go to college, he was sent to the Oxford philosopher T. H. Green, who was married to his aunt Charlotte, to be taught enough to get into Balliol.

This brought about some improvement, but he still failed the preliminary Mods examination twice, and was sent down to be an external student until he passed it, which he managed to do the following year. He was then permitted to switch to History, which he greatly preferred, and from which study he learnt to believe in Free Trade, a cause he supported for the rest of his life.

He was not popular with his contemporaries or with the dons, as he was thought to show off, and was later mocked by Roger Fry in the style of the famous series of verses in the Masque of Balliol, which included the one about the Master Jowett:

> First come I, my name is Jowett.
> There is no knowledge but I know it.
> I am Master of this College,
> What I don't know isn't knowledge.

The verse about St Loe ran:

> I am Strachey, never bored
> By Webster, Massinger or Ford.
> There is no line of any poet
> Which can be quoted but I know it.

All his life he remained a constant quoter, even to the extent of irritating many people by the habit.

St Loe, on his side, disliked Jowett and his snobbery in making favourites of students whom he hoped would succeed in life—among whom he clearly did not include St Loe.

On leaving Oxford St Loe was intended for the Bar, but it soon became clear that he was going to be a journalist instead. The owner-editor of the important Liberal weekly paper *The Spectator* at that time, Meredith Townsend, was a friend of St Loe's father, Sir Edward, who was a frequent contributor to the paper, and he soon became a friend too.

He had been brought up in a broadly Whig atmosphere, and though a firm Imperialist, he too saw himself as a convinced Liberal. When the Gladstone controversies on the subject of Home Rule for Ireland arose, however, he came down against

Home Rule and on the side of the Unionists. He also opposed Chamberlain's Imperial Preference in favour of Free Trade. He found himself, therefore, opposing the policies of both parties, and unable to be wholehearted in defence of either—not, as his grandfather Sir Henry had found, a good basis for a successful political career. St Loe stood only once for Parliament, for the Scottish Universities, and was not elected.

Instead of becoming a politician, he decided to exert his independent influence by means of the Press.

At that time *The Spectator* was the most important political paper in the country, and was more influential and more widely respected than any periodical today. All the articles were unsigned, and St Loe strongly supported the principle of anonymity, believing that it encouraged impartiality and discouraged vanity. Nevertheless it was not long before his name was known and he was highly regarded for his editorials, and when Meredith Townsend came to retire, St Loe was invited to succeed him as Editor.

To obtain complete control over what he published, he determined to buy the paper, too. He did not have enough money himself, though Sir Edward had passed on his sons' inheritances in advance, but his brother Henry lent him virtually all his own capital to make up the sum. The two brothers were very good friends, and St Loe later made Henry Art Editor of the paper.

Not content with *The Spectator* alone, in 1901 St Loe bought a paper called *The Country Gentleman*, because, he said, it was on the way to his office, and he could not bear to pass every day the window of a paper in which he had no hand. He got his brother Henry to design a new cover, and Amy wrote for it, as St Loe felt that it would smack of favouritism if she wrote for *The Spectator*, even anonymously. It was never, however, a financial success.

St Loe complained that he could not safely make friends as he might be forced to comment adversely on anyone at any time, but in fact he had many, including the remarkable explorer, Mary Kingsley, who would entertain the family with hair-raising tales of her adventures in the African jungle, and Evelyn Baring, later Lord Cromer, for more than twenty years British Agent and virtual ruler of Egypt, whose views on Empire, 'To govern always in the interests of the governed,' exactly tallied with those of St Loe.

St Loe had married Amy Simpson, granddaughter of Nassau Senior, the first Professor of Political Economy at Oxford. They had three children, Tom, a delicate boy, who died of pneumonia at Oxford in 1906, Amabel, who married the architect Clough Williams Ellis, designer of the fantasy village of Portmeirion on the coast of Wales, and who became a prolific writer, and John Evelyn, named for Lord Cromer and his godson.

St Loe had a great love and admiration for America, and conducted a long private and political correspondence with Theodore Roosevelt, from the time Roosevelt was Governor of New York State through his Presidency and afterwards. In 1902 the Stracheys went to America, and to their great satisfaction were guests at the White House: Roosevelt returned the visit to the Stracheys in 1907.

In addition to his love of literature of all sorts, St Loe was always interested in military affairs, and followed the Boer War closely. He was no Pacifist, and not pro-Boer, indeed he held a more Tory than Whig position on overseas affairs, believing with Cromer that 'Orientals were not yet fit for self-government'. He was also in favour of 'Battle Spirit' though he denied saying that 'without War the race would deteriorate'.

During the Edwardian era *The Spectator* and St Loe became increasingly influential. The Free Trade campaign the paper ran between 1903 and 1905 caused Chamberlain to regard it as one of the great obstacles to his policy of Tariff Reform. By 1909, however, there were new trends in the Liberal party which St Loe liked even less. He came out strongly against Lloyd George, who retaliated by calling him 'an exceedingly pretentious, pompous and futile person'. On his side St Loe said that he regarded himself as a watchdog. 'I have a right, nay a duty', he wrote, 'to do my best to bring the Will of the People in accord with what I hold to be right, just, and likely to promote the welfare of the Nation.'

As time went by, the threat of a European war, which he was convinced would come before 1920, loomed ever closer, and St

Loe formed a plan to train civilians in rifle-shooting as a protection against invasion. This was on the lines of the Home Guard in the Second World War, but was not officially supported. He succeeded in building up village rifle clubs throughout the country without any Government help or finance, and when war finally did break out, his lists were found to be most valuable, as they contained the names of 30,000 to 40,000 trained men, prepared to serve overseas or at home. He went on to work in other ways for recruitment, while his home at Newlands Corner became a hospital and his wife worked for the Red Cross. His patriotic feelings were, as were those of so many people at the time, inflamed by the war, and he wrote: 'If the English speaking world is to take the lead and to bring mankind out of the shadows once again into the light, it can only be through care, toil and sacrifice'—a somewhat jingoistic version of Churchill's later and more celebrated saying.

Concerned, as ever, for Anglo-American relations, particularly in Press matters, he also started a scheme for informal, off-the-record tea-time meetings of American correspondents with men in the Cabinet and other important positions, such as the Archbishop of Canterbury, to counter the oppressive and, in his view, stupid Censorship regulations. The Government was very much against this at first, for security reasons, but St Loe's personal connections enabled him to persuade the Prime Minister, Asquith, to come to the first meeting, and a fruitful series of exchanges resulted.

After the war St Loe's health began to deteriorate, and he died in 1927. Although his style of thought was now beginning to sound distinctly outdated, and his more Bohemian cousins stigmatized him as pompous and 'Spectatorial', he was still active. He was captivated in the early twenties by the emergent Mussolini, but nevertheless remained sufficiently open-minded not to be unduly distressed when his son John Evelyn decided to become a Socialist and join the Labour party. John, a brilliant writer and speaker, became in due course Minister of Food and Secretary of State for War.

John's politics, however, enraged St Loe's elder brother Eddy, now Lord Strachie. He could not bear the thought of a Socialist inheriting Sutton Court, and so he persuaded his daughter's husband Lord O'Hagan and their family to take the name Strachey, and left the house to them, happy that both the name and the house would thus be preserved.

INDIA AGAIN

Henry Strachey and his brothers, William and George

(1816–1912)

Henry, the second son of Edward and Julia, born in 1816, was destined for the Army in India. He went to Addiscombe, the Company's military academy, rather than Haileybury, was posted as an Ensign in 1835, to the Gurkhas, and proved himself to be, like his ancestors, quick at learning oriental languages. He had also shown an early talent for mathematics and a great love for architecture, which, had he not gone to India, he would have taken as his career, a love which persisted all his life and which he himself called 'a mania'.

In India he worked at first as an engineer on the construction of the Grand Trunk Road between Fatehpur and Allahabad and then on the construction of the Kulubdia Lighthouse on the Chittagong coast.

Smitten after this by the common Indian affliction of recurrent fever, in 1846 he went up to Almora in the Hills on sick leave and as he recovered decided to explore the nearby Himalayas, pushing up through the passes to Tibet and returning with a great deal of new and valuable scientific and political information. He had no financial help for the expedition and he had a tough struggle with the Tibetan border guards before they would let him into the country.

The journey at that date was a very difficult and risky one. Henry travelled light, in local costume and without European companions, and his excellent results were due, it was reported, to his 'proficiency in the native languages and close and friendly intercourse with the inhabitants'.

Tibet had very rarely been visited by Europeans at that time and such maps as existed were based on surveys by Lamas or an early Chinese report with maps drawn by Jesuit missionaries in Peking in 1717.

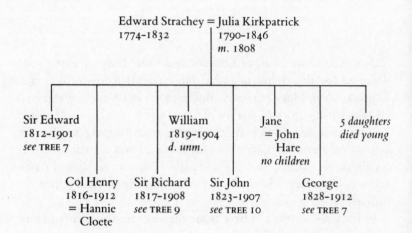

Edward Strachey = Julia Kirkpatrick
1774-1832   1790-1846
m. 1808

Sir Edward
1812-1901
see TREE 7

Col Henry
1816-1912
= Hannie
Cloete

William
1819-1904
d. unm.

Sir Richard
1817-1908
see TREE 9

Sir John
1823-1907
see TREE 10

Jane
= John
Hare
no children

George
1828-1912
see TREE 7

*5 daughters
died young*

FAMILY TREE 8

A Tibetan grammar—also compiled by Jesuits—was published in 1762. These sources and the reports on the Tibetan explorations of Moorcroft in 1812 were virtually all that was then known: there were, for instance, no triangulated peaks in the West Himalayas to guide him. Henry's expedition produced the first accurate reports about the mountains, together with an excellent series of maps and sketches, and was followed by two expeditions in 1848 and 1849 by his brother Richard.

Meanwhile in 1847 a recovered Henry was appointed a member of the Kashmir Boundary Commission, and again explored the Himalayas and surveyed Ladakh country as far as Leh, but was prevented from going further this time by Chinese opposition.

He returned to England in 1851 and travelled for a time in Europe, determined to seek out and enjoy a feast of architectural beauties.

While he was in Paris, the Royal Geographical Society awarded him their Victoria Gold Medal for his explorations and surveys, and Richard, who was then also in Europe, received it on his behalf in his absence.

The great era of Victorian exploration was only just beginning; it was ten years before the start of the famous expeditions to discover the sources of the Nile, but Henry's travels caught the imagination of the country, and he became for a while almost famous. These undiscovered areas of the globe came to arouse the same kind of excitement as in this century has been aroused by the exploration of space and the moon.

Henry returned to India in 1855, but was forced to take sick leave again four years later, and this time was sent to South Africa, like his grandfather, William Kirkpatrick. There he met and married a South African girl called Hannie Cloete. Their only child, a daughter, Julia, who married Sir William Chance, was an artist, particularly fond of drawing cats.

Henry retired from India in 1861, and for a time acted as agent at Sutton Court for his brother Edward. Though hampered by increasingly poor sight, for as long as he could he went on studying and enjoying architecture.

With later and fuller explorations the importance of Henry's early discoveries naturally diminished, but they were not forgotten. The great Swedish explorer Sven Hedin proposed in 1910 that the mountain range in the Himalayas 'bordering the very uppermost part of the Brahmaputra' be called the Strachey Range, after Henry and Richard. 'As a rule,' he wrote, 'I hate European names on Asiatic maps. Wherever native names are to be found, no other should ever be used. But in some cases, and for lack of native names, it may be useful and practical to introduce exotic ones. And as far as Tibet is concerned, no names have a greater right to appear on the map than those of Montgomerie, Strachey and Ryder.' A range was, in fact, named after Ryder, but none after Montgomerie or Strachey.

Henry went entirely blind when he was 83. He lived on, however, till he was 96, and though the second of the brothers, was the last to die. Two of the six lived to be over 90, while the youngest to die was 84.

William, the fourth brother, and George, the youngest, were both eccentrics; William was the oddest of them all, and there are many family stories about him. He was a bachelor and though he went into the Indian Service in 1838, at the usual age of nineteen, he only spent five years there, and then made his way home to London, where, according to his brother Richard he was 'going to bed at 3 am and getting up at 2 pm in a whirl of fashionable life, and almost invisible'.

He finally resigned, to work for some years in the Colonial Office, and while there it appears he was chosen for special work from time to time by Palmerston, though of what kind there is no record. Thereafter he would take every suitable or unsuitable conversational opportunity to remark: 'I remember Lord Palmerston used to say to me. . . .'

Short as his stay in India had been, it had convinced him that the only 'trustworthy' time was Calcutta time, and he lived by this in England for the remaining 56 years of his life, breakfasting at teatime, lunching at midnight, and, like Lewis Carroll's Snark, dining on the following day. Breakfast, moreover, he preferred to eat standing, and off the mantelpiece, where it was laid for him, and he liked his eggs cold. He finally took almost entirely to the nocturnal life and was rarely seen.

At the time of the Great Exhibition he underwent a temporary urge to return to a more normal timetable. He therefore bought a bed which had been advertised in the Exhibition and which threw its occupant out at a predetermined time. The first time he used it, it threw him into the bath-tub placed (for some reason) beside his bed, whereupon he broke the thing up in a rage and reverted to his normal habits.

When he arrived in England he had put up at a small and elegant hotel with his valet, Joseph. Not intending to stay more than a few nights, he told Joseph to leave the trunks downstairs. In fact he stayed there for more than 30 years, but the trunks were never taken upstairs, and Joseph had to extract anything he might want and carry it up to his room for him.

He was definitely a man of the world, and a great dandy in his own eyes, never leaving the house without galoshes and continuing to wear the much buttoned fashions of the 1850s, at which time he was a member of Brooks's Club, and a friend of Thackeray.

Whenever he went to Sutton Court, which he would do without announcing himself, he would drive out from Bristol station in a cab. If, as frequently happened, he would be arriving at dinner time (though of course this would be nearer breakfast time for him) he would change into evening clothes in the cab on the way, with the blinds pulled down.

The local people in Somerset believed him to be an astrologer, and the family doctor was inspired to say that Stracheys would never go mad, they were too eccentric.

George, too, was odd, but not quite so colourful; an enigmatic and retiring man who loved music and played both the piano and the 'cello. He had helped to edit the school paper at his prep school, and sent a copy to Carlyle, who provided kindly praise, thus clearly nurturing the conviction in George's breast that he was cut out to be a journalist.

He did not go to India, but into the Diplomatic Service. He became an Attaché at the Embassy at St Petersburg and later in Vienna and The Hague, and finally became Resident Minister at the court of Dresden, where he remained for 30 years.

He kept up his journalistic ambitions, and wrote almost as

many articles for the more serious periodicals as his brother Edward, but though their content was often interesting, his self-conscious and long-winded style makes them virtually unreadable today.

He married twice, his first wife being his first cousin Georgiana Strachey, daughter of Richard of Ashwick Grove, whom he carried off under the nose of his elder brother Edward. She died of a miscarriage and inflammation of the lungs a year later, and though deeply affected, he married again. Lionel, one of his sons by his second wife, emigrated to America, and there in his turn became a writer and journalist, contributing, like other Stracheys, to the family paper, *The Spectator*.

SERVANTS OF INDIA

Richard and John

(1817–66)

Richard, the third son of Edward and Julia, who was born in 1817, and John, the fifth son, who was six years younger, were extremely close friends throughout their lives. They not only both went to India, but frequently lived together and worked together in complete harmony, while their wives were first cousins. They were both knighted for their services to India, and both were highly intelligent, highly critical, first-class administrators, and complete and open agnostics in an age when conformity, if not belief, was almost universal.

Richard was physically the stronger and the more versatile. He soon showed outstanding mathematical ability and left Addiscombe, the military academy of the Company, as head of his class. He was due to be given the Sword of Honour, but could not resist openly criticizing the Drill Sergeant, a want of discipline which caused the Sword to be given instead to the second on the list. After Addiscombe he became a Lieutenant in the Bombay Engineers, soon transferring to the Bengal Engineers.

At that time India had virtually no decent roads and bridges had only just begun to be built. Railways, starting with the East India Railway, of which Richard was ultimately to become Chairman, were first proposed for India in the 1840s, but prejudice and controversy delayed them, until ten years later following energetic pressure by Lord Dalhousie, the then Governor General. Irrigation works, too, were only just being started, and Richard was sent to the head waters of the Jumna and the Ganges Canal, one of the Government's first large-scale efforts in that direction. There were very few English officers there, and Richard worked like a navvy himself, in his shirtsleeves.

In 1846 the British army moved into the Punjab to suppress fighting among the warlike Sikhs. Richard, on the Jumna, was

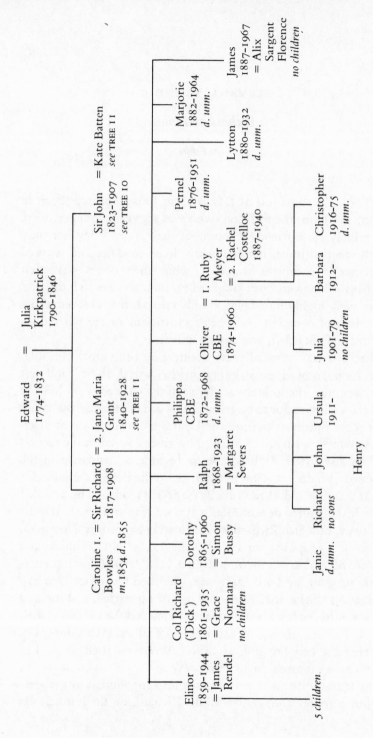

FAMILY TREE 9

within earshot of the firing, and he and the other officers engaged on the works set off across country at once, to join Sir Harry Smith's Division.

He took part in the battles of Aliwal and Sobraon, in the First Sikh War, and wrote describing them afterwards to John.

We saw the Sikh force drawn out in front of their camp across the low ground; we advanced till we got within range of their guns when they opened fire upon us and made an elegant row and dust. The whole of their line was however forced. Our loss is not great, considering the results. . . . I had my horse shot through both legs nearly at the beginning of the affair, I had gone to order our guns to advance and was standing alongside them; I fortunately got hold of a troop horse and rode him for the rest of the day.

After Aliwal the army began to feel more confident, from the C in C downwards. I dined at the C in C's in the capacity of one of Sir Harry's Staff. Just as we sat down Abbott of ours appeared—he had been sent from Ferozepoor by the Governor General to invite the C in C to attack. . . . In the evening the Generals and Brigadiers were assembled and matters were explained to them. The attack was supposed to be a secret till the time, but of course every rascal in camp knew of it from the commencement.

This was to be the battle of Sobraon, also a victory for the British. At one stage Richard came across a Cavalry regiment stationary when it should manifestly have been advancing. When he asked why, the colonel fumed that he could not move without orders from the Staff. 'I am one of the Staff', said Richard, 'and I order you to move on at once'. Whereupon the Colonel thanked him profusely and advanced with speed.

Richard drew the authoritative plan of the Sikh position, and with his friend Baird Smith (who had been given the Sword of Honour Richard's critical nature had lost him) he threw a bridge across the river Sutlej to enable the troops to pursue the enemy.

Although he finished his career as a Lieutenant General, this was in fact the only time Richard was involved in actual fighting—his talents were too useful elsewhere—but he proved himself a good soldier, and Sir Harry Smith reported of the two young Lieutenants that they were ready to act in any capacity, and called them 'two most promising and gallant officers'. Richard was awarded a medal with clasp, and soon afterwards received promotion to Captain, with his Brevet Majority the next day.

Back on the Ganges Canal he began to suffer from recurrent attacks of fever, and was forced to transfer to the Hill station of Naini Tal. Here he made good friends with Major E. Madden, from whom he enthusiastically learned botany and geology.

When his brother Henry returned with reports of his adventures in Tibet, Richard too determined to explore the Himalayas, which he had seen and admired from Naini Tal, and he set off in the summer of 1848 with a friend called J. F. Winterbottom, on a scientific plant-hunting expedition.

The two were successful in collecting, and scientifically labelling and annotating, over 2,000 species, many of them hitherto unknown and of the greatest botanical importance. Thirty-two species bear Richard's name, including the unique *Stracheia Tibetica*.

Botany, however, was not the only subject Richard studied and observed. He also assembled geological, geographical and meteorological material and information on watersheds, altitudes, snowfalls, and the nature and position of the sacred lakes in the mountains, illustrating his report with accurate maps and attractive sketches. The extent of his material and the detail of its presentation, according to the Royal Geographical Society, 'has never been exceeded by any one traveller'.

There were less strictly scientific discoveries, too. One of the first Europeans to report on it, he noted with considerable amusement the repulsive taste of Tibetan tea with rancid butter and the hideous appearance of Tibetan women—who were not, he felt, entitled to be called 'The Fair Sex'. Richard's children, however, loved best his story of how, when climbing along a narrow ledge, he put his hand round a projecting rock and met the hairy paw of a large bear. Both he and the bear were clearly taken aback, and paused. When asked what happened next, he

LT. COLONEL HENRY STRACHEY,

Col. Henry Strachey
(1816–1912) by
Henry Strachey

William Strachey
(1819–1904) on the
terrace of Sutton
Court, 1902

Jane Maria, Lady Strachey (1840-1928)

Richard Strachey (1817-1908) as a young man,
by M. Yule

Sir John (1823–1907) and Sir Richard Strachey, 1876

Sir Richard Strachey in middle age, by T. Blake Wirgam

Lady Strachey in old age *c.* 1920

would reply: 'The bear was the greater gentleman; he retreated and I followed.'

The Himalayas, not surprisingly, made an enormous and lasting impression on him, and he is reported to have said that until he saw them he was an atheist, but afterwards an agnostic.

After a further mountain expedition with his brother Henry the following year, he returned to England and stayed there for almost five years, living and working with Winterbottom on the enormous task of cataloguing their botanical collection.

Meanwhile John had followed him out to India in 1842, as a civilian. John was a spidery man with floppy black hair a moustache and spectacles, never as strong as Richard, though certainly comparable in intelligence. His physical type appeared again and again among the Stracheys, and John, his three sons, and two of Richard's sons were, to judge by the photographs, very similar in appearance.

At Haileybury John had won prizes for everything from classics to political economy, and did well, in the family tradition, in Persian language and literature. He passed out second on the Company list for Bengal, and worked there for some years as a District Officer.

At home, Richard's friends were almost all scientists, closest of all, perhaps, being T. H. Huxley. In 1854 when he was 37 he was elected a Fellow of the Royal Society for his various scientific discoveries and the same year he married a girl called Caroline Bowles, daughter of a clergyman in Malvern. They had hardly reached India in the following year, however, when Caroline caught a fever, had a miscarriage, and died.

Richard was now posted to the Department of Public Works, while John was a District Officer in Allahabad. Here he was assistant to George Batten, member of another leading Anglo-Indian family, whose daughter, Kate, he married in 1856.

There was a great deal of intermarriage, not surprisingly among these Anglo-Indian families, as the English in India were then called. There were very few of them; the Indian Civil Service, which provided the senior men in the Administration and the Judiciary, numbered no more than 916 by 1870, to cover the whole subcontinent—of whom only one, incidentally, was an

Indian—and only about 40 were appointed every year. These few, moreover, were very scattered, and social life very limited. To see anything of their husbands and yet bear and rear their children safely in those medically primitive times, the wives had either to separate themselves for many years from their children, or to accustom themselves to the constant gruelling journeys out from England and back, which only became more tolerable by slow degrees, as first the railway from Alexandria to Suez and finally the Canal itself was opened. They also had to endure the climate and the loneliness and the inevitably high deathrate, and a wife brought up to the life was likely to be happier and healthier—as well as easier to find—than one who had never left England. As a result of these marriages there came to be a small, close and very gifted class of top Indian administrators, just as there was a comparable class of Indian army officers, almost all of whom were related to each other, by blood or marriage.

John used to call Richard 'King Richard' and both he and Kate had a great respect as well as affection for him. In almost all his letters to his brother John would call on him urgently for help, to get him clothes, candlesticks, a revolver, plaster busts, chintz and advice of all kinds, adding to all these requests, 'You *must* send this quickly,' or, 'I will hate you deadly if you don't send this by return of post'. He was rarely in good health, but though both he and Richard were openly critical of people they considered fools, John was always the more vehement of the two. In his private affairs, however, he was a great ditherer and found it almost impossible to make plans and stick to them—an odd contrast to his fierce decisiveness in his work.

Early in 1857 Kate was pregnant and John's health was again bad, and he came home to England with her. It was a busy year in the family, with Sir Henry's death, the quarrel between Edward and George over George's marriage to Georgiana, and Georgiana's death, within a year of the wedding, and Edward's wedding to Maribella Symonds. With the outbreak of the Mutiny, however, events in India took immediate precedence.

John made strenuous efforts to get back there at once, but was not yet considered fit. 'Whether sitting in England doing nothing does or does not do me good is doubtful,' he wrote to Richard. 'Perhaps it does, but *liking* it is different and I wish I was back.'

He was not to return until the end of the following year, but was then noticed by the authorities, and by 1862 he was moving into top posts, Chief Justice of the Central Provinces and President of various Commissions.

When the Mutiny broke out Richard was Under Secretary in the Department of Public Works, under John Peter Grant, whose wife was Kate Strachey's aunt. Richard was determined that there should be efficient systems of transport and irrigation in India, and the fierce way he went about it brought results but he was, as his colleagues put it: 'neither conciliatory nor popular'. Those who fulfilled his strict requirements of ability, hard work and intelligence, however, found him both invaluable and congenial, and he never lacked good friends.

As the Mutiny raged on, John Russell Colvin, Lieutenant Governor of the Northwestern Provinces was beleaguered in Agra, and John Peter Grant was sent to the capital of the province, Allahabad, which was on the edge of the disturbances, to prevent them spreading eastwards to Calcutta, bringing with them, in all probability, famine and pestilence. Grant took Richard with him to act as Secretary in all departments and they managed to preserve peace in the province. While there, he was faced with a subordinate who rushed in to tell him that mutineers were about to pour into the city and all that remained to them was to rely on Providence. Richard snapped back that this was always a disastrous thing to do, and he had better take steps himself.

1858 saw the official transfer of the control of India from the East India Company to the British Government, and there was a brilliant round of celebrations. Grant, for one, now President of the Council in Calcutta, gave a vast ball, for which Richard, the engineer, organized splendid illuminations with thousands of oil lamps in earthenware pots. Grant's wife, the beautiful Henrietta Chichele Plowden, and several of their children were also in India at this time, and Richard met them at their summer house in Naini Tal and fell in love with their younger daughter, Jane Maria.

There was a big difference in their ages; Janie was only eighteen and Richard 41, but this was quite common at the time, both in India and in England. Janie reported that the first time she saw him, in evening dress, small, black-haired and beak-nosed, sitting on a yellow sofa, he looked just like a wasp—a not unfitting description. Two months later they were married.

Janie like Richard was descended from Anglo-Indian families on both sides; she had been born in a sailing ship on the way home, in a storm off the Cape of Good Hope, and was well prepared for the difficult and unsettled life she would have to lead. She was 5 foot 10 inches tall, half a head taller than Richard, big-boned, blonde, shortsighted, a little ungraceful and modest about her appearance. Richard, however, greatly enjoyed her quick and humorous intelligence, and assured her that she looked like a duchess. He called her his 'Sweet cat' and their children were her 'kittens', and signed himself, as she did to him, all their lives, 'Your devoted . . .' or sometimes 'Your physicky cat'.

John Peter Grant was now appointed Governor of Bengal, in charge of more than 70 million people, and when her mother returned to England with the younger children, Janie became, for a while, the senior lady in Calcutta society, a position she much enjoyed. Together with the Viceroy, 'Clemency' Canning, Grant was, however, extremely unpopular in England, where anti-Indian hysteria was rife, and their efforts to apply impartial justice had resulted in their being accused of favouring Indian mutineers above British soldiers. Grant's family had even seen him lampooned on the stage in London.

The Government, however, took a more favourable view of his efforts, gave him a KBE and, when he came home soon afterwards, appointed him Governor of Jamaica, charged with healing the resentment caused by the harshness of the previous Governor, Edward Eyre.

In 1860 Richard, now a Lieutenant Colonel, had fallen ill again, and had to return to England for a year, rejoining the Department of Public Works in Calcutta just as Sir John Peter Grant retired. He worked as Consultant Engineer of the Railways and First Inspector of Irrigation, he fought vigorously for the founding of a forestry service, urging its importance for agriculture, meteorology and his beloved railways, and became head of the department.

Richard was critical of Lord Canning, and accused him of *laissez-faire* in government policy and in Public Works in particular, but he found his successor, Lord Elgin, more congenial. 'I go to Lord Elgin every Thursday, at ten o'clock a.m. to do the work', he wrote to Janie. 'He is very civil and obedient.' He was aware that his fierceness and energy made him enemies; he was even too radical for his father-in-law. 'I shall become stronger than ever', he wrote on his return to India, 'as I shall be the only person who knows anything or has any ideas about Public Works. I shall not shrink, my sweet cat, from driving the coach my own road.' 'I sometimes fear', he added however, 'that the world must think me rather meddlesome. But it cannot be helped, dear Janie; if we are to go on, somebody must lead, and why not I as well as another. . . . Now you will say that this is Strachey insolence, and so it is—but it is for all that mixed up with another ingredient of Strachey blood, that is modesty.'

India was governed at that time by a Secretary of State in the London cabinet, advised, primarily on financial affairs, by 10 to 15 members of the India Council. This was made up largely of men who had served in India, appointed for five or ten years. In India itself there was a Viceroy, who also had his Council consisting of an Inner Supreme Council of six members and an outer group of Heads of various departments. No member of the Inner Council at that time was expert in, or responsible for the decisions in the field of Public Works, and Richard therefore had direct access to the Viceroy and unique influence, which he used then and later to great effect.

When Lord Elgin died in harness, he was succeeded by one of the greatest of the Viceroys, Sir John Lawrence. Richard found him a most satisfactory chief and Lawrence in turn approved equally strongly of both Strachey brothers. 'Lawrence', wrote Richard, 'is abrupt and forcible [both qualities of which he thought highly] and is not particular to a shade in what he says in private to me.' He added, however, that he was spartan and hard, and must be stood up to and 'regularly ground up'.

The expansion of public works in India in the 1860s was to a considerable degree due to Richard's forceful efforts. As John later wrote of his brother: 'It is to him that India owes the initiation of that great policy of the systematic extension of railways and canals which has been crowned with such extraordinary success, which has increased to an incalculable extent the wealth of the country and has profoundly altered its condition.' Not only was it responsible for the expansion of trade and industry, but it also enabled effective action to be taken against famine and the spread of cholera, and was among the most important of the material advances brought by British rule.

It was perhaps the railways on which Richard put the most importance, and when funds could not otherwise be obtained for financing them he pushed through permission to do so by means of floating loans. He drafted the vital despatch to be sent to the Secretary of State in London by the Viceroy, demanding that this course be followed, and laying out all the arguments and figures, and when he took it in to Lawrence to be signed, the Viceroy put his 'L' at the foot of the document without changing a word and said, with a grin: 'Strachey, they will think me very clever!'

Richard's love for Janie, strengthened by their repeated separations, continued to be passionate. 'When you are gone,' he wrote, 'It is all darkness, and what is possible but to burn up? And when you come back, after one great eruption of fire and flame, I shall again become the quiet gray mountain that looks as though it could do nothing good or evil.'

Janie was starting what was to become a very large family. Three of the thirteen children she bore died in infancy, one of them called Caroline after Richard's first wife. Ten grew to adulthood, five boys and five girls, and the last child was born when Richard was 70 and Janie 47.

For much of the time Janie had been living in Simla. The Government had just started to move its senior members up there officially for the hot weather, which meant that husbands could see more of their wives. Richard still had a great deal of travelling to do, however, inspecting his public works on the spot, and Janie lived meanwhile in a large, agreeable square house called the Yarrows, where she was a great organizer of amateur theatricals and an energetic dancer. As a soldier's wife, she was bold, too, and one day when a leopard dashed across her verandah, she dashed after it (in vain) with a croquet mallet.

Richard's letters show that he had a very high opinion of Janie's intelligence and good sense. He encouraged her to learn mathematics and philosophy and it is clear that she shared his scepticism about religion. He remarked once of a shipboard fellow-passenger in a letter to her, that he was 'one of the pious Barnet lot' who 'though inclined to be fair, had extreme difficulty in perceiving that it might not be the duty of Government to insist on having the Bible read in all Indian schools.' John, too, was fiercely agnostic and once remarked, 'What a damned thing piety is. The longer one lives the more forcibly this truth impresses itself on the mind.'

Richard took greatly to Positivism and the philosophy of Comte, though he regarded him as 'a true intellectual genius with a complete want of balance of faculties of a practical nature'. 'I perceive', he continued, 'that the tendency of my own education and instinct has been to exalt unduly the value of the sciences of number and quantity—mathematics. It is not very easy to get rid of a habit of thought such as this, but even now it is perhaps not too late to correct such things.' And a few days later: 'I have got into such good habits of rational discussion with you that I feel quite uncomfortable from not having anyone who will take an interest in my speculations. I go on rather feebly with Comte, but require your sparkling sauce to make it properly enjoyable.'

Despite his promotion to a full Colonelcy, which assured him a more reasonable pension than had appeared likely after the amalgamation of the Company's army with the Army proper, there were increasing financial problems. In 1865 he had decided to retire and settle down in England, but the failure of the Bank of Agra the following year, in which almost all his funds were lodged, forced him to go back to India for paid work for another five-year period. John, too, was badly hit by the loss, and wrote to Richard saying that his fate now depended on his health being good enough for him to stay on, as otherwise he would be ruined.

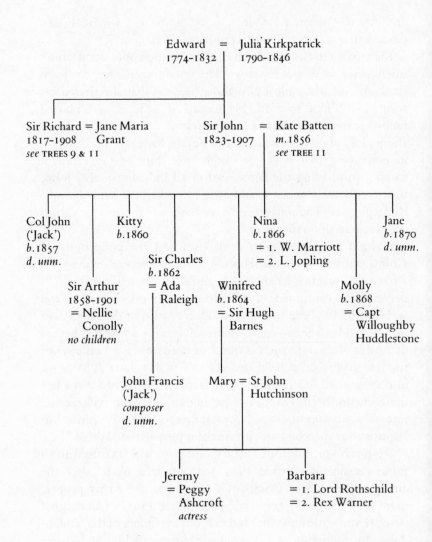

Edward = Julia Kirkpatrick
1774–1832 | 1790–1846

Sir Richard = Jane Maria
1817–1908 Grant
see TREES 9 & 11

Sir John = Kate Batten
1823–1907 *m.*1856
see TREE 11

Col John ('Jack')
*b.*1857
d. unm.

Kitty
*b.*1860

Sir Arthur
1858–1901
= Nellie
Conolly
no children

Sir Charles
*b.*1862
= Ada
Raleigh

Winifred
*b.*1864
= Sir Hugh
Barnes

Nina
*b.*1866
= 1. W. Marriott
= 2. L. Jopling

Molly
*b.*1868
= Capt
Willoughby
Huddlestone

Jane
*b.*1870
d. unm.

John Francis ('Jack')
composer
d. unm.

Mary = St John
Hutchinson

Jeremy
= Peggy
Ashcroft
actress

Barbara
= 1. Lord Rothschild
= 2. Rex Warner

FAMILY TREE 10

THE STRACHEY RAJ

Richard and John

(1866–1908)

On his return to India in December 1866, Richard again became Secretary of the Public Works Department, where his first concerns were irrigation and railways. He put in hand plans for a barrage on the river Indus, despite local incredulity, obstruction and delay, which would double the revenue of Sindh in the following ten years, and he achieved outstanding results on the railways in building bridges and extending and improving the lines. The East India Railway now stretched for over a thousand miles and was making a healthy profit.

Meanwhile Lawrence, who was nicknamed 'The Poor Man's Friend', had made John Chief Commissioner at Oudh, with instructions to try to reach an equitable solution to the land settlement problem. John did what he could and achieved agreement, but he left it on record that he had been unable, owing to previous rulings, to do as much for the tenants as he would have wished—indeed he feared the agreement might have made things worse for them.

Two years later he was called to Calcutta as Finance Member of the Supreme Council.

Now that they were both in Calcutta, John and Richard began to live and work together. Richard, according to John, was the originator of their plans, and John the operator. They had three main ambitions for India: to expand the communications system until it was adequate to handle all requirements; to end the inefficient system by which all provincial financial decisions were referred to the central government with resulting friction, delay and incompetence, and lastly to rationalize the incoherent weights and measures, to introduce the metric system and to reform the currency, prevent inflation and facilitate foreign trade. They put much importance, too, on overall economy, a necessity in view of the fact that the rupee was starting to fall. Exchange rates between the various Indian currency values and the pound were at any time almost impossible to compute, and there was endless scope for corruption. Weights and measures, too, were different in every district, but despite the obvious advantages of standardization the immense and age-old inertia of India, which together with the debilitating climate caused too many English officials to resent the introduction of any change, even for the better, finally prevented their being entirely successful.

In the railway system, Richard fought for years what came to be known as 'The Battle of the Gauges'. Dalhousie had been well aware of the vital importance of fixing one gauge for the whole country, but that used in England at the time was four feet eight and a half inches while five feet six inches was agreed for India. This turned out not to be practicable for many of the branch lines in mountainous country, and was opposed in the 1860s for reasons of economy. Richard wanted a uniform two foot nine inch gauge, but this was thought to be too narrow, and the Viceroy, Lord Mayo, anxious to achieve agreement, decreed a compromise three feet three inches, which meant that more than one gauge had, in the end, to be used. The best Richard could manage was to act like a belated fairy godmother at a christening. As he wrote to his father-in-law: 'Lord Mayo was afraid of two feet nine inches as being too small and wanted to make a sort of compromise between the very narrow and the rather narrow at three feet six inches. So he took three feet three inches and I added ⅜ inch to make up the metre. On the whole it will do very well and will stamp the metre on the face of India very nicely.'

To alter weights and measures was even more difficult. There were local rivalries of all kinds, and the British objected to the metre as being French, while to impose the almost equally chaotic English measures would have been futile. Richard, well in advance of his generation, drafted an Act introducing a uniform metric system, and actually got it on to the Statute Book, but it was impossible to implement. Only after Independence was it brought into force, when the Indian Government gave full credit to Richard's foresight.

Their financial reforms were in the end more successful,

though the provincial governments, particularly that of Madras, deeply resented the brothers and considered them dictatorial. As Richard, in true Victorian style, wrote to Janie: 'He who insists on that which has been done ill being done well or better must be looked on as offensive. . . . There are few "spirits of elite" who can simply abandon wrong with satisfaction and pass over to right. Let us cultivate such a frame of mind, dearest wife, in ourselves and our children.'

The upbringing of the children was, as can be imagined, not easy, but Janie's sister, Elinor Colville, took in those who were left at home, and Janie and Kate took over the rest for each other in turn. Richard was a fond father and wrote frequently and affectionately to his family, while referring to them collectively as 'creatures'. They were all, including Janie, great puzzle addicts, and in that pre-crossword age Richard regularly made up and sent them acrostics to solve. He was regarded by all the family as the one to fall back on. He looked after the school and later college arrangements and supervised the financial and disciplinary dealings not only with his own children but also with John's and with Janie's younger brothers in the absence of their father in Jamaica. The boys seem to have given a good deal of trouble one way or another. Janie's brother Jack, for instance, ran heavily into debt at one stage, and her favourite brother, Trevor, outraged local society by marrying a Eurasian girl who was, said Richard, neither engaging nor wise, and whom Trevor would never bring home to meet the family. They had four sons, one of whom was expelled from school, and one, according to family tradition, hugged to death by a bear.

Both Richard's and John's eldest sons—Dick and Jack respectively—were less than entirely satisfactory, too. Both went into the Army but were, by Victorian standards, idle and spendthrift. When Dick failed to do well in his army exams, Richard was disappointed and wrote: 'If he has any faculties that are likely to lead to much good they are still in the condition of simple protoplasm. I don't think there is much appearance of the Strachey tendency being carried on into the future through my offspring. Perhaps the world has had enough of it.' In the end Dick became a competent though not outstanding soldier, and the 'Strachey tendency' though it certainly changed direction with his later children, could not be said to have entirely disappeared.

Janie joined Richard in Calcutta in 1868 with her three-year-old daughter, Dorothy, who acted as bridesmaid to Sir John Lawrence's daughter. She now found herself involved in the fascinating business of real power, for Richard and John drafted most of the Viceroy's important despatches and orders, and these were first shown to Janie and her suggestions frequently followed. On one occasion a paragraph she had rewritten caused Richard to exclaim: 'What a clever old beast you are!' and the Duke of Argyll, then the Secretary of State for India, later read it out in Parliament, commenting, 'After such an expression of opinion as this from the Government of India, how could the India Office do other than accept their policy?'

As Richard wrote when she had returned to England: 'Dearest cat, it is some consolation in the wilderness to feel that one is helping on the cause of reason and civilization, and to me in particular, that what I am trying to do is the fruit of thought and discussion in which you have taken no small part.'

John and Richard were still unpopular with their colleagues, however, and they became known as 'The Strachey Raj', 'Castor and Pollux' and the 'Bouncing Brothers' by their enemies. The Indian periodical, *The Pioneer* wrote in January 1871:

Of the five ordinary members of the Council Mr John Strachey, says a native contemporary, ranks first, and of the seven additional members his brother Colonel Richard Strachey also occupies the same rank. These two brothers constitute at present the leading members of the Council and the main strength of the Viceroy. They are an exceedingly clever pair, and because so clever, their influence is the more to be dreaded, there being no equal or higher element in the Council to counteract it.

Richard was the one, as John admitted, who had the greater initiating impulse, but his post as Secretary of the Public Works Department did not carry a seat in the Inner Council and only the

Viceroy and his close associates knew the full extent and nature of his influence.

The stronger Viceroys, such as Elgin and Lawrence, had welcomed this influence. Lawrence had put him forward for Finance Member before appointing John to the post, but Richard's critics in the Home Government refused to accept him. Finally when it became clear that Public Works must be represented in the Inner Council, and that the obvious man was Richard, it was the then Viceroy, Lord Northbrook, who declined to appoint him.

The fact that this was due to personal dislike on the part of Lord Northbrook was evident, and was underlined by the Duke of Argyll who wrote from London to tell Richard of the refusal and to offer him at the same time a post on the India Council in London, who acted as advisers to the Secretary of State.

Richard made it clear that if this situation continued he would have to resign, and when he was offered the post of Inspector of Equipment for the Indian Railways, in England, he did resign, in 1872, at the age of 54, hoping for a quiet life at last, little realizing that his career was in fact only half over.

Life was not always so serious, however. Janie told of how Richard and John were shut up together one day, in consultation on a very important matter. 'Several callers on official business arrived', she went on, 'and all were asked to wait until the consultation should be over. After a considerable time had elapsed, the Private Secretary ventured cautiously to enter the room. There he beheld the two great statesmen busily and silently engaged in winding up the favourite black cat with red tape. The animal was quite calm and composed.'

John stayed on after Richard left—his time on the Council did not come to an end until 1873, but his health was getting worse all the time and he brooded over the possibility of going home sooner. The Viceroy, now Lord Mayo, was unhappy at the prospect; it would, he said, be very difficult to find a suitable substitute. John continually urged Richard to return to India, but without success.

In 1872 the Viceroy, Lord Mayo, was assassinated by a convict in the Andaman Islands, and John, as senior member of the Council, acted as Pro-Viceroy until the arrival of his successor, and was given a Knighthood.

He was, however, nearing a breakdown. 'I utterly loathe and abominate the prospect of staying in India', he wrote, but when he was offered the better paid and less demanding post of Lieutenant Governor of the North Western Provinces, based on Allahabad, he accepted. Here he was able to think of other things than money for a while. He took the first active steps to preserve the great monuments of Agra, the Tomb of Akhbar and the Taj Mahal, and strongly supported the Muslim College at Aligarh, where a Hall was named after him.

He also built a new summer Government House at Naini Tal, in the Hills, and sited it high above the rest of the town. Sir Alfred Lyall, a later—but still pre-motor-car—Lieutenant Governor, said that he 'felt savage at Strachey every day' for building it so far away from the town and all its amenities. He assumed that John had had three reasons for this choice: 'To see the snows', 'a sort of tyrannical caprice' and 'because he liked doing singular and remarkable things'. There may well have been much truth in this, but John and Kate were not of a very sociable turn of mind, and greatly enjoyed their isolation. As Kate complained: 'I nowadays positively dislike so-called gaieties, balls etc.'

John's eyesight was fading. 'My belief is', he wrote to Richard in 1875, 'that I shall never see out of my right eye again. Further it seems very probable that if I go on using my left eye as I have hitherto been doing, it will follow its blessed brother's example.' He scarcely slept, and not surprisingly took a jaundiced view of life. 'I thoroughly detest the forms and ceremonies of a Lieutenant Governor's life', he wrote, but he couldn't decide to give up the post without getting something comparable at home.

Meanwhile a further social trial was in store for him. During the winter of 1875–6 the Prince of Wales paid a long visit to India and John and Kate were required to entertain him and his suite. Kate wrote to Janie: 'It is a literal truth that *we* shall have to entertain the Prince for a longer time than anyone in India, Viceroy included. Luckily the Viceroy tells John confidentially, by desire of the Secretary of State, that after it is all over he must say privately what it has all cost him and that the money will be reimbursed. Otherwise we should have gone to jail.' This was at least an advance on the days of Good Queen Bess's expensive visits.

Even so it was a struggle. Kate called on Janie for linen and Richard for crockery. 'I am giving you a great deal of trouble,' she apologized, 'but I cannot help it, it is all the horrid Prince.'

In the event it was not so bad as they had feared, though he did indeed stay with them not only in Allahabad where the Viceroy was also of the party and the grounds were full of tents for the overflow guests, but also at Agra, Benares and the Hills. Kate had found one of his suite 'a coarse oafish creature' and another 'a horrible coarse looking man who drinks brandy and water all day'. They also drank 'between seventy and eighty dozen of champagne in a fortnight and fourteen dozen of soda water in a day'.

They were less critical of the Prince himself. 'We bade a final farewell to the Prince the other day,' she wrote in March 1876. 'He has behaved very well with us. John curses and swears directly his back is turned, but admits when he is present in the flesh he is so goodnatured and polite and *likeable* that one can't help liking him.'

Lord Northbrook had resigned, and in April 1876, a month after the Prince departed, the new Viceroy, Lord Lytton, arrived. He had been briefed by James Fitzjames Stephen—brother of Sir Leslie, the father of Virginia Woolf. Stephen had been Legal member of the Council from 1869 to 1873, and had made lasting friends with both John and Richard. As a result of his advice Lytton stopped over at Allahabad on his way to Calcutta, to consult John. 'I don't suppose', John reported to Richard, 'that in any previous 24 hours I talked so much as in these—at an early stage of the proceedings Lord Lytton told me that he had come to India with one predominant hope—that I would consent to be his Finance Minister.'

John and Lytton took to each other at once. Lytton was a man of great charm and culture. He wrote poetry as Owen Meredith and was fully as eccentric, and in the end, as unpopular, as the Stracheys. He was handsome, warmhearted and informal;

lounged in his chair at receptions, ran out into the street in his pale-blue dressing-gown, refused to go to church and had no taste for protocol. Wilfred Blunt★ who was visiting Lytton wrote in his diary; 'I have seen him walk up and down for a quarter of an hour together with Sir John Strachey, his Finance Minister, his arm round the man's neck, a really amusing spectacle, for Sir John, a bilious and elderly official in spectacles, with his head habitually on one side, was more like a sick raven than an object of endearments of any kind, and their talk was of figures and the revenue.'

John had hesitated before agreeing to return to the Council. It meant a considerable drop in salary as well as more demanding work. He finally managed to get a sum of £5,000 agreed as compensation, but, as he told Richard, some of this would be deducted if he left early, so he would have to hang on.

Famine in the south of India was now the most urgent problem, the worst calamity of its kind since the beginning of the century. John, now 55, became even more urgent in his efforts to get Richard to come out and help him, and finally the opportunity arose. Richard was asked to go out and supervise the sale of the railways to the Indian Government, who, now that they were beginning to make money, had decided to take up their contractual right to purchase. He only expected to be out there for a few months, but Lord Lytton came to visit him the very day he arrived, and said that he was in misery at the thought of John's going, but he had been warned by his doctors that he must rest. It was a great relief to get Richard instead, though he feared that Richard would be tougher with him. Richard realized that he was doomed to stay.

The famine provided a way of giving him an official status until his replacement of John could be agreed in London, and he was made Famine Commissioner. It was no easy post. There was much controversy about how to deal with the emergency. Bombay, taking the line advised by John, though it was tougher and less 'charitable' than many people thought desirable, had been

---

★ Wilfred Scawen Blunt, traveller and poet, married to Byron's granddaughter, with whom he bred Arab horses.

more energetic and efficient in pushing their Public Works programme for distributing relief, and their mortality was therefore much lower than that of Madras. The Governor of Madras, the Duke of Buckingham, was an obstinate man. John had never thought much of him and had once written to Richard cheerfully that he had 'nearly been used up through his horse rearing'. He was now insisting on handing out charity without safeguards and much of it never reached the sufferers.

Richard was tactful on this occasion, as well as firm, and a Famine Code was finally worked out which was to operate efficiently for decades. As Richard wrote to his father-in-law: 'Famine has to come . . . and until it has come possibly more than once, the only practicable remedy—provision of irrigation and improved means of communication—will not be applied. In this respect the world is unaltered, our progress, such as it is, goes over dead men's bones and is forced down the throats of the wise men and patriots of the day.'

Once officially agreed and installed as acting Finance Minister, Richard sent for Janie, writing to her before she came: 'Till now I have *never* been in a position to exercise real power, and I have a little hesitation in assuming it. I . . . think that it is probable, if the occasion actually arises, that I shall be more disposed to *consult* my colleagues than John has been. I will not say anything as to taking their advice if I don't like it. He has been for a long time in a position of actual authority and has got used to it. I have already seen that in a large class of subjects Lord Lytton will be wholly guided by what I may say—if I remain here—and that it is not only myself that I become responsible for, but for him also, and the Government of India.'

John returned to Europe for a year at the end of 1877, and spent most of this time in Italy. Lord Lytton wrote to Stephen: 'His courage is indomitable and if he were stone-blind he would still see further, clearer and quicker than any other man in India. But I feel very unhappy about him, not only because he is my ablest adviser, but also because I love him as a true friend.'

Lytton also came to be very fond of Richard, and above all Janie, with whom he corresponded regularly until his death in 1891, keeping her up-to-date in matters of state—in an indiscreet way. When he left India he would ask her criticism of his poetry and discuss literature and drama, to which they were both passionately addicted. He also acted as godfather and namesake to her fourth son, Lytton.

In 1878 Lytton became involved in the disastrous campaign in Afghanistan to which he had been impelled by the Tory Prime Minister Disraeli. This war was highly unpopular in almost all quarters in England. Both the Stracheys and their wives were radicals, but their friendship for Lytton nevertheless led Richard to support him in the Indian Council.

In January 1879 John returned, somewhat improved in health, and Richard and Janie went back to England, where he was again appointed to the London Council of India, this time for life—a unique privilege.

John plunged at once into work on the Budget, writing to Richard by every mail, reporting progress, asking advice and urging his support with the Secretary of State and the London Council. He was still balanced between fear and hope of early retirement. As he wrote in May: 'I think it would be a capital plan if I were recalled. It would not make me in the least unhappy and we would go straight to Bellosguardo.' But at the same time he was frantic to finish his work first. He succeeded in completing Richard's plan for equalizing and reducing the Salt Tax, and removing the ruinous customs barrier which had stretched across the whole country, and began to work for the long overdue reorganization of the Military Department and its finance. This involved trying to get rid of its head, Edwin Johnson, who was failing and of whom he wrote: 'He sets his face against every suggestion which aims at change of any sort . . . it is impossible to doubt that last year's attack has had a serious effect on him. He appears well enough in health but his incompetence cannot be exaggerated.'

Of the Military Department as a whole he said: 'Its inefficiency has become really scandalous. It is not too much to say that there is no Military Department at all.'

Johnson did finally ask for leave in November, but not before the department's shortcomings had brought disaster both on Johnson himself and on John.

In September the ill-fated Afghan expedition had ended in Kabul in massacre and failure, and in March 1880, amid strong Parliamentary censure, the government fell, and Gladstone became Prime Minister. Lord Lytton resigned at once.

The following month he wrote to Janie: 'My impression is that the malcontents in the Home Council who have been fuming and fretting at the establishment of the Strachey policies will take advantage of unprecedented difficulties for a stronger attack.'

A month later the blow fell. It was discovered that the estimates for the Afghan War had been too low by no less than twelve million pounds, and that the actual expenditure was seventeen million pounds—more than three times as much as the estimate. John's budget reforms had been so successful that almost all the difference could be paid out of revenue, but the discrepancy was too great to be passed over.

The miscalculation was due to the defective system of accounts used by the Military Department, but John's criticisms had not been implemented in time.

Johnson, of course, had to resign. Kate wrote to Janie: 'If abominable accusations are made of John deliberately falsifying accounts and telling lies then we should go away with the Lyttons, but it would be most inconvenient from every point of view.' And a fortnight later:

How unfortunate it has been, this mistake in the war estimates. . . . I don't know if you see any Indian newspapers, but the very violent charges and abuse and the ugliest motives attributed, have been showered upon John and Lord Lytton. John says he does not care a 'tinkers' but though I try to argue with myself against it, I *do* care. . . . John is coming to the conclusion that the system of military accounts in India is altogether rotten and that no particular individual is to blame for what happened. The great temptation is for him to resign, but I feel sure that it would not do, at any rate now. If he did, people in England would be sure to say it was a confession of weakness and that the Government could not support him so he was obliged to resign.

She did, however, admit: 'He could only accept the estimates given to him by the responsible department. Perhaps as they were so good, that ought to have made him suspicious.'

John chose to resign and went to live in Italy, where he was a convinced and ardent supporter of the Risorgimento and wished, with typical combativeness, that he could have fought with Garibaldi.

Instead he produced, in conjunction with Richard, a clear and admirably written book on the Finances and Public Works of India, laying out the problems they had been presented with and the solutions the 'Strachey Raj' had worked out for them. In the preface he wrote:

This book is the joint production of my brother and myself. For many years we have taken part, often in close association, in the Government of India, and it would be a false affectation of humility to profess that this part has not been an important one. There is hardly a great office of the State, from that of Acting Viceroy, Lieutenant Governor or Member of the Council downwards, which one or other of us has not held, and there is hardly a department of the administration with which one or other of us has not been intimately connected.

The book came out just before the Indian Budget was declared, a budget which would carry out almost all the Strachey plans. John wrote jubilantly to Richard:

About the middle of February it will reach India, and all the newspapers will be exulting over the failure of the brothers to carry out the whole of their plans, which were declared so unblushingly in this book. A fortnight afterwards comes the Budget. I don't think Baring* and his friends will half like the position and it cannot be denied that it is somewhat embarrassing for them. However much they desire to take all the credit to themselves it will be very difficult for them to do so. If

* Evelyn Baring, later Lord Cromer, was then Finance Member of the Council.

a longer time had elapsed between the appearance of the book and the Budget, their absolute adoption of all our plans might seem less patent.

Three years after leaving India John returned to England and was appointed to the London India Council for ten years, to join Richard. As time passed he wrote a treatise in defence of Warren Hastings in the Rohilla War, and gave a series of lectures on Indian History at Cambridge. In June 1907 he was given a DCL by Oxford, and in December he died, two months before Richard.

Both brothers spent their lives and risked their health to provide good government and material prosperity for the people of India, but they were nevertheless very isolated from the actual life of the country. Richard was much in favour of social contact between English and Indians, but living and working, as the brothers did, in the upper ranks of central administration, such contact was virtually non-existent, and there is no mention of any in their letters to each other or to their wives. Their lives, apart from the Indian sights and sounds and problems around them, and the hundreds of Indian servants, was—in contrast to that of James Achilles Kirkpatrick for instance, almost wholly English.

A LONG CAREER

Richard

(1817–1908)

It was not only in the administration of India that Richard made his mark.

In botany his contributions were great, not only in the numbers of new plants that he and Winterbottom had discovered, but also in the scrupulous and invaluable detail with which he charted the conditions in which he found them. This included logging heights of up to 18,000 feet which, he said, he had found perfectly tolerable 'if you were not too energetic'. He had taken virtually no instruments—only thermometers, a barometer, a small theodolite and an azimuth compass, together with 'a few bundles of paper for drying plants'. At the date of his Himalayan journeys there was of course no photography, but he was a meticulous and gifted draughtsman, and illustrated everything.

In 1873 he was appointed to the Managing Committee of Kew Gardens, and there and in the Royal Society his close friend and colleague was Joseph Hooker, the botanist. He travelled with him in the South of France in 1874, and three years later he took Janie with him on a long excursion in the United States with Hooker and Professor Asa Gray, to inspect parks and botanical gardens throughout the country.

They were to form the botanical branch of an official survey party in the West, and travelled by train, paddle-steamer and on mule-back, camping in the mountains, making explorations and surveys. Janie greatly liked Boston and much enjoyed the whole adventure, particularly the camping, but she reported that she found the Rockies 'somewhat diminutive' after the Himalayas. She was more impressed when they reached Salt Lake City and called on Brigham Young, who looked, she thought, highly intelligent, but in person exactly like a family butler.

Richard and Janie were unable to get as far as California with the rest of the party, as Richard was due to sail for India on railway business, on the occasion when he was later to replace John as acting Finance Minister.

In 1884 Richard and Janie again visited America, this time staying in Washington, DC. Richard was one of the three delegates chosen as Secretaries at the Conference which agreed on Greenwich as the prime Meridian line and the basis for worldwide Time Zones. A system for fixing time had been sought for centuries, and had become increasingly urgent with the arrival of railways, which made a common basis for timetables essential. Richard, as always, was before his time in insisting that before long a 24-hour timetable would also be needed, for railways if for nothing else.

All the countries at the conference except France and one very small state of Mexico welcomed the choice of Greenwich happily, but the astronomer Jansson, who was the French delegate, was violently anti-British, and was extremely rude, which made Richard's task a difficult one.

Richard had long been a member of the Royal Geographical Society, and was made President for two years in 1887, and an Honorary member of the Geographical Societies of Berlin and Italy. Of his own work for the Society it was said that he showed 'a keen determined face and instant decision. There was no "uncertain sound" about Sir Richard's opinions'. He never hesitated to speak his mind, either, and of one member with whom he disagreed he wrote in a report: '. . . .'s geography, if it deserves the name, is perfectly worthless', and of a speech by the explorer Stanley that it was 'insulting to those who think of Geography as I do'.

In 1888 he was invited to give a series of lectures at Cambridge on geography, in the same year that John was lecturing there on India, and he was forthright and uncompromising, as usual, in standing up for geography as a subject to be taught and respected.

In 1889 he resigned from the India Council on being appointed Chairman of the East India Railway, and also of the Assam Bengal Line, whose construction he had directed—two lines which were thereafter known in the family as the Hee High Har and the Hay Bee Har. Richard at once travelled out to India with the Chief Engineer of the EIR, Sir Alexander Rendel whose son had married his eldest daughter, Elinor, to make searching enquiries into conditions and management. Despite his age (he was 72) he brought in a new and more active regime. His status with the Government enabled him to stand up to them, and he fought public opinion and competition from the Welsh mines to support the use of his line in the coal trade. He pushed on the construction of more branches and local lines; he introduced express trains, and he founded a school for the children of employees. He went on working—and working actively—as Chairman, attending the office several days a week and staying until six o'clock or later, until he was 90, when increasing deafness drove him to resign, a few months before his death. He had received a salary of £1,000 a year, but there were no arrangements for a pension, and the drop in income forced the family to move to a smaller house. As a tribute to his services, however, a few weeks before his death a new railway bridge was opened in Agra, which bore, and still bears, his name.

Meanwhile in 1892 he attended the World Monetary Conference in Brussels as delegate for India, and was at last able to welcome the reform of the Indian currency and the end of free coinage of silver which he had recommended fifteen years previously, and the knowledge that the losses caused by the delay had at last been brought to an end.

Perhaps his most important scientific work was done in the field of meteorology. Before 1860 this had been a most primitive and uncertain field, and Richard was largely responsible for working out the early scientific methods adopted. He was a member of the Royal Society's Meteorological Committee, and Chairman of the Council, for twenty years, starting in 1883, when he was already 66 years old. He also did much for the foundation of the study in India, where he was particularly concerned with the forecasting of droughts.

He was always very active in the Royal Society; four times on the Council and twice Vice President. He thought more highly of his Fellowship there than any of the numerous other honours he had received. He had refused a knighthood five times, although offered by five successive Secretaries of State for India. Finally it was felt that the only way of getting him to accept would be to grant it without consulting him in advance. As Janie explained: 'On the morning of the Second Jubilee, after opening the *Times*, I carried it into Richard's dressing-room, where he was shaving. "You are gazetted G.C.S.I. (Grand Commander of the Star of India)" said I: he turned round with the razor in his hand, and ejaculated "Rubbish!" He did not mean that the title was rubbish, but thought I was joking. It was really a great surprise, for he had five times refused to be nominated for the K.C.S.I.'

The Royal Society gave him their Gold Medal—the highest scientific honour in the country—in the same year. At the committee meeting at which it was discussed there was much argument over which of the sciences he had pursued should figure in the citation for the medal, until finally his good friend, T. H. Huxley, broke in, saying, 'Oh well, let's just give him the medal for being old Strachey.'

He was also given the Symons medal of the Meteorological Society for his report on the barometrical disturbances after the great eruption of Krakatoa in 1888, which led to important discoveries about drift in the upper atmosphere.

His dictatorial manners were still often resented. The Indian press, which had never forgiven him, wrote on his appointment as President of the Geographical Society: 'In the snug harbour which he has found for himself . . . although he still clings to some of his old crotchets, much of his former asperity has been smoothed down. If he wishes for controversy he can find it from day to day in the Government Meteorological Office, of which he is the chief.'*

His colleagues there did not agree with this. He had, they said, 'clear insight, perfect lucidity in thought and expression and logical marshalling of facts in all documents'. They added that 'he had not much patience with people who were imperfectly acquainted with the facts of a case under discussion and he never cared to argue with them, but difference of opinion on lines of policy, even when ill expressed, never ruffled his serenity'. It was popularly said, incidentally, that he did not have a waste-paper

* Homeward Mail 25 July 1887.

basket in his office, as he never had to correct anything he wrote.

At home Richard was a different man. John was known for his bad language in private, but Richard was always (or nearly always) calm and reasonable. His family knew him as sweet-natured and most affectionate; he was happy to play bears with the children, and was even useful about the house, fitting up his own bells, for instance, or cutting out his wife's dresses.

He was not, however, forthcoming outside the circle of his intimates. As he said himself, when he met General (then Colonel) Gordon at Gosport in 1861: 'Colonel Gordon is very dry—though I dare say very good. His husk is very thick, and I not being myself very demonstrative or talkative, make a bad hand at amusing him.'

He was very tolerant for a Victorian, approving of his wife's considerable and vehement activities on behalf of women's suffrage, and holding a moderate, if stable, view of manners and morals. 'I am not a Puritan,' he said, 'but I like to see young ladies regard their "forms".' He argued with Janie—but without heat—against Bohemianism, of which he did not approve, but which she held could be valuable.

He remained a sceptic to the end. 'It seems to me', he wrote to Janie, 'that a person can only absolutely and completely realize his *own* convictions, and that, more particularly in such a sceptical being as me, everything that belongs to the internal existence of another being must be a little doubtful.' And later: 'I understand life, with all its wonderful offshoots of thought, volition, motion and so on, to be a *condition* of matter, just as heat or light is a condition. When that "life-condition" ceases, the phenomenon as a *whole* ceases absolutely.'

He was born in the reign of George III and died at 91, six years before the First World War, in February 1908, having enjoyed an active working life of over 70 years.

'DEAREST CAT'

Richard's wife Janie

(1840–1928)

Jane Maria Grant was born on a sailing ship in a storm off the Cape of Good Hope, a fact which might be seen as a pointer to the kind of life she was to lead, at least while she was young. It was to be a life full of travel and action, and scarcely ever at rest.

Both her parents belonged to the small group of Anglo-Indian civilian families, including Grants, Plowdens, Battens, Stephens and Stracheys, having traditional links with India and with each other that reached back for generations.

Her father, John Peter Grant, was a Highland Scot, of Rothiemurcus, near Aviemore, and her mother, Henrietta Chichele Plowden, was a great beauty. She had two sisters, Elinor, who was older, and Henrietta (Henny) who was younger and mentally retarded. There were also five brothers.

From the very beginning Jane had to accustom herself to living in boarding houses, to sudden uprootings and to frequent, long, uncomfortable journeys, as the family shuttled between England and India, or up to Rothiemurcus by stage coach. At the time of her birth, the trip round the Cape of Good Hope took some five months, as it had in the days of Clive. Fifteen years later, with the coming of the railways, this was shortened to a matter of weeks. First the travellers went by train to Naples or Brindisi and then by ship for the comparatively short crossing to Alexandria. Thence by coach at first, and later by train, they continued to Suez, where they embarked for Bombay or Calcutta. Finally with the opening of the Suez Canal, the ships were able to go straight through, and the journey took no more than a week or two.

Wives of the more junior officials often spent years on end in India, but those who could afford it tended to travel back and forth in this way every few years, so as to keep in touch with their children. These tended to arrive every year, some born in India,

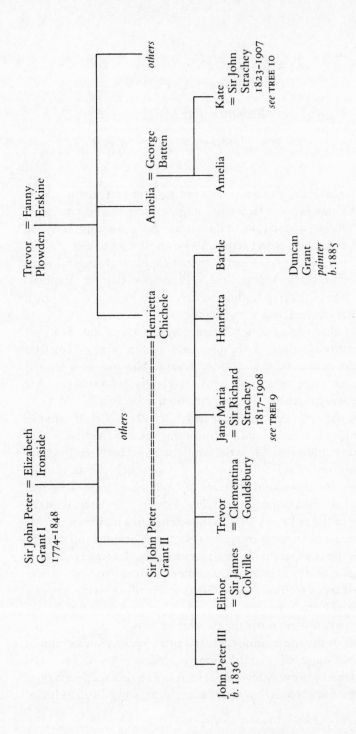

FAMILY TREE II

some in England, and the little ones were often taken out for a year or two. When they reached school age, however, or sometimes younger, they stayed in England. The arrangements necessary for all this movement and separation were made possible by the close and affectionate relationships in their large families. Aunts and sisters took the children in, and their children, in turn, were housed and cared for at one end or the other, or accompanied *en route*. There was never a shortage of such shelterers, and Janie, in later life, still found it natural and pleasant to live among a horde of relatives and to feel sadly lonely and deprived if she was not able to welcome large numbers of them to her home every Sunday.

In India, whether in the cities or the plains or in the hills in the hot weather, there were always many servants of all kinds. The majority of English families employed an ayah to look after the children, who were often inoculated thus with an early knowledge of the language and a love of the country which would serve them well later on. There were worries too, however, in this course, as it often meant that the children were hopelessly spoilt and suffered extra risks of infection. Some parents, including Richard Strachey, were strongly against leaving an ayah in sole charge. Richard urged Janie to bring out an English nurse, even though they were aware that this was a considerable responsibility. Sometimes the girls could not bear the life, sometimes they got married at once, and sometimes they proved incompatible and had to be sent back and replaced, at considerable expense.

Illness among the children was, in any case, always a threat. Even more than at home they infected each other and a horrifying number died, as can be seen from the tombstones all over the country. The Stracheys were comparatively lucky. Of the thirteen children Janie bore Richard Strachey, the second daughter, Caroline, died on the journey out, a few days before reaching port, and another daughter, Olivia, died in England of scarlet fever. Only one actually died in India, an infant son called Roger.

Janie was a capable organizer but was unwilling to be tied down to domestic preoccupations. She was always a voracious reader, both in English and in French, and had inherited much of her mother's passionate love of music. Richard, when he married her, found her both intelligent and intellectual, and took care to encourage this. He urged her to learn mathematics, but realizing his own impatience suggested that she find another master until she had made enough progress to avoid irritating him. He discussed with her not only his work but also his thoughts. 'I have got into the habit', he wrote in 1867, 'of indulging in intellectual talk with you and I find that I can't bring myself to the level of the world in which I now generally am.'

Janie's most particular love was for the theatre. Amateur theatricals played a large part in Anglo-Indian life at that time. In 1880 Lord Lytton spent £2,000 (which he could ill afford) on theatricals at Government House, Calcutta, and fitted out a theatre in Simla specially for amateurs, and Janie and her cousin Kate were both very active in this line. She developed the art of reading aloud—now, alas, almost lost—and was famous among her family and friends for her highly spirited (if somewhat bowdlerised) readings of Elizabethan and Jacobean drama. All her children were brought up on large doses of both French and English literature.

One aspect of her life was far from ideal and that was the perpetual house-moving. In 1873, with help from her father, Richard finally bought a house on Clapham Common, which they called Stowey House, after the village near Sutton Court, and there they managed to stay for no less than twelve years. 'This was the first time in my life', Janie wrote, 'that I had ever spent more than two years in the same house.'

More children were still arriving, five here and one more in their next house at Lancaster Gate. One of these was called Pernel, and Kate wrote that she supposed the name had something to do with Janie's perennial babies.

Once settled in England Janie was able to be more active in her own concerns. She had never liked housekeeping, and was not at all good at it, though she was always a most loving and protective mother to her large brood. She had been a keen feminist from the age of nineteen, since reading John Stuart Mill's *On Liberty* in 1859, and had helped to circulate the first petition to Parliament for women's votes. She was a great friend of Dame Millicent Fawcett, leader of the law-abiding, non-suffragette feminists, and regularly marched at the head of processions, wrote pamphlets and organized fund raising. Her third daughter, Pippa, spent her life working for the same cause, a canny strategist and expert lobbyist, and was finally awarded the C.B.E. for her work.

Richard had always done what he could for the rights and freedoms of Indian women, and sympathized fully with Janie's feelings on the subject, though he reserved the right to tease her at times. Once, when travelling by elephant on one of his inspection tours he wrote: 'I often think that I should wish to have you with me as I am going along, and consider how you could climb into a Howdah, which would be a difficult operation with petticoats. There is another disability of the sex!'

He was extremely proud of the scholastic successes of his daughters. He did not live to see Pernel become Principal of Newnham College, Cambridge, but when she first went there in 1895, passing the stiff entrance examination with credit, after being coached by her elder sister Dorothy, he made a proud little speech to the assembled Council of the Meteorological Society.

Janie's friends were mostly in literary and musical circles, though she found her husband's scientific colleagues, George Darwin, Hooker, Huxley and Galton, even more fascinating, so she sometimes said. The 'cellist Piatti once dedicated a song to her, while the great violinist Joachim was a close friend and constant visitor, and his photograph hung in her front hall for years. She had first read Browning in Simla in 1863, and at once wrote to her sister Elinor of her admiration and delight. Elinor replied that she was just about to dine with him, and Janie was so envious that she wept. When she got back to England, however, she made good friends with him herself, as she did with George Eliot, with whom she used to indulge a joint passion for the theatre. But perhaps the literary friend to whom she was most devoted was still Lord Lytton, who frequently asked her for suggestions and criticism of his poetry written under the name of Owen Meredith.

She sometimes wrote herself, too, but not really very well, and oddly enough, mostly bad verse of a rather sentimental kind. She also edited the interesting memoirs of her aunt, Eliza Grant Smith of Baltiboys.★

She had always been very shortsighted; all her children, inheriting poor sight, as they did, from both sides, wore spectacles, and two of them suffered from detached retina, as she did later in life herself. In 1917 she had to have her left eye removed, and she later went almost completely blind. She had always had a passion for puzzles, which she had passed on to all her children; she particularly loved jigsaws, and did not see why she should be deprived of them by a little thing like blindness. She therefore had a board made with stand-up rims, and had all the pieces turned over the right way and laid out for her so that she could put them together by touch.

In the war her third son, Oliver, who was my own father, was employed at the War Office as a cryptographer, and was asked to suggest other suitable recruits for the work. Janie at once applied, and was furious when she was turned down, ascribing it— although she was already over 70—entirely to anti-feminism.

She lived on after Richard's death, first in Hampstead and then in Bloomsbury, until 1928, still vigorous in conversation and argument, though no longer able to read the books she loved.

★ *Memoirs of a Highland Lady*, edited by Lady Strachey, Murray, 1898.

Epilogue

After the end of Queen Victoria's reign the family connection with India began to die away. Only Arthur, John Strachey's second son, fully followed the family pattern. He was born in 1858, became a much-loved Chief Justice of the Court at Allahabad, was knighted, and died in 1901, at only 43.

John's eldest son, Jack, and Richard's eldest son, Dick, both became Colonels in the Indian Army, competent but not outstanding soldiers, while John's third son, Charles, was also knighted, and served in the Foreign Office and the Colonial Office, but dealt with Africa, not India. Charles had one son, Jack, who startled the family by becoming a composer of popular songs, including *The Tailwagger's Anthem* and the evergreen *These Foolish Things Remind Me Of You.*

John's family was older than Richard's. He too had five daughters, but all but one of them married and moved away from each other and the rest of the family, although one granddaughter, Mary Barnes, who married a lawyer called St John Hutchinson, moved in Bloomsbury circles for many years.

Two more of Richard's sons did indeed work in India. Ralph became Chief Engineer of the East Indian Railway, and Oliver, who had wanted to become a pianist, but found that he had neither quite enough talent nor nearly enough diligence, was finally found work on the Railway too. He hated it, however, and bitterly missed the artistic and intellectual life at home. Having married and divorced a beautiful but flighty girl he met there, he returned thankfully to England for good in 1911 and married again.

The new century and the new reign brought a change of emphasis in the family outlook and direction. Richard's children were no longer, like their ancestors, administrators with intellectual tastes and friends, but intellectuals all through.

Lytton Strachey is the best known, but he was not the only one to achieve distinction. Five of Richard and Janie's children, together with a daughter-in-law and a grandson, were to be found in *Who's Who:* Colonel Dick, Philippa, who was given a C.B.E. for her feminist work, Oliver, who was also given a C.B.E. for his work as a cryptographer through two world wars, Pernel, Principal of Newnham College, Cambridge, Ray Strachey, Oliver's second wife, who worked with Philippa and became a leader in the Suffrage movement, as well as a writer, and their son, Christopher, first Professor of Computing Science at Oxford.

In addition to these, Dorothy, the second daughter, married a French artist, Simon Bussy, became André Gide's translator and wrote a delicate study of adolescent emotion called *Olivia* which was later filmed, while the youngest son, James, studied with Freud and became a psycho-analyst and Freud's editor and translator.

Lytton is known not only for his books, which introduced a new and irreverent style of biography, but also for his deliberately disruptive effect on the conventions and preconceptions of the Victorians. This naturally aroused a good deal of disapproval at the time, when many Victorians were still alive, but the people he loved and respected, both his family and the circle of friends who came to be known as Bloomsbury, shared his beliefs and standards, and while they were never uncritical, their criticism was informed and affectionate.

There are now, sad to say, very few male Stracheys left to carry on the name. Some emigrated to New Zealand, where they flourished, and some to America, where they lost touch, but in England, even including the senior, O'Hagan, family, Stracheys by name can be counted on one hand. There have been shrinkages and resurgences in the family history before, however, and perhaps, in an era of better medical care, one of those surviving will again produce a crop of 15 or 18 offspring to build up the line and carry on the type.

Sources and Selected Bibliography

Throughout this book I have relied on *The Strachey Family* by C. R. Sanders, Duke University, (1953), *Materials for a History of the Strachey Family,* assembled by Sir Edward Strachey, Sir Charles Strachey and St Loe Strachey, privately printed by *The Spectator* (1899), and also on the *Dictionary of National Biography* and the *Dictionary of Indian Biography* covering the various people concerned. I have also included material derived from verbal family tradition.

All books were published in London unless otherwise stated.

Prelude and Chapter 1   The Merchant Venturer: William Strachey (1450–1621)

A. *Manuscripts*

CULLIFORD, S. G., Unpublished Thesis on William Strachey for the University of London, University of London Library (1950).

STRACHEY, WILLIAM, Mr Strachey's 'Hark', Ashmole Collection, Bodleian Library (c. 1620).

B. *Printed Material*

BULLOUGH G., *Narrative and Dramatic Sources of Shakespeare* (1975).

CAWLEY, R. R., *Shakespeare's Use of the Voyagers*, Boston (1926).

   First Folger Series, ed. Louis B. Wright and Virginia La Mar, Ithaca, N.Y. (1962).

GAYLEY, C. M., *Shakespeare and the Founders of Liberty*, New York (1917).

HARBAGE, A. B., *Shakespeare and the Rival Traditions*, Bloomington, Indiana and London (1917).

HOTSON, L., *'I, William Shakespeare, do appoint Thomas Russell, Esquire'* (1937).

SISSON, C. J., *New Readings in Shakespeare* (1961).

SMITH, CAPTAIN JOHN AND OTHERS, *A Map of Virginia, with a description of the country*, Oxford (1612).

STRACHEY, WILLIAM, *A True Reportory of the Wracke and Redemption of Sir Thomas Gates, Knight, upon and from the Islands of the Bermudas*, ed. L. B. Wright, Charlottesville (1964).

—— *A History of Travaile into Virginia Britania*, ed. L. B. Wright and V. Freund, (Hakluyt Society, second series, ciii, Charlottesville (1953).

WALLACE, W., *The Children of the Chapel at Blackfriars*, Nebraska (1908).

Chapter 2   Sutton Court, William of Camberwell to Henry of Edinburgh (1621–1764)

A. *Manuscripts*

Strachey papers, Somerset Record Office, Taunton.

B. *Printed Material*

COLLINSON, J. A., *History of Somerset* (1791).

FOX BOURNE, H. R. F., *Life of John Locke* (1876).

KING, P. (ed.), *Life and Letters of John Locke* (1889).

RAND, B. (ed.), *The Correspondence of John Locke and Edward Clarke* (1927).

Chapter 3   In India with Clive: Henry Strachey (1732–74)

A. *Manuscripts*

Ormathwaite Collection, India Office Library and Records.

Powys Collection, India Office Library and Records.

Strachey Collection (Sir Henry Strachey), India Office Library and Records.

Diary of Jane Latham, 1768, India Office Library and Records.

B. *Printed Material*

BENCE-JONES, M., *Clive of India* (1974).

COTTON, H. E. A., 'Clive and the Strachey Family', *Bengal Past and Present*, XXVII.

FRANCIS, SIR PHILIP, *Memoirs*, ed. Parkes and Merivale (1867).

GARDNER, B., *The East India Company* (1971).
STRACHEY, SIR E., 'The death of Clive', *Spectator* (4 August 1883).
WEITZMAN, S., *Warren Hastings and Philip Francis* (1929).
WOODRUFF, P., *The Founders* (1953).

Chapter 4   The American War: Sir Henry Strachey (1774–1810)

A. *Manuscripts*

Ormathwaite Collection, India Office Library and Records.
Strachey papers (Sir Henry Strachey), India Office Library and Records.
Strachey papers The William L. Clements Library, University of Michigan, Ann Arbor.
Strachey papers The George Bancroft, Rare Books and Mss. Division, The New York Public Library, Astor, Lenox and Tilden.

B. *Printed Material*

ADAMS, J. Q., *Memoirs*, vol. III, ed. C. F. Ada, Philadelphia (1874).
BAILEY, T. A., *A Diplomatic History of the American People*, New York (1941).
GRUBER, D., *The Howe Brothers* (1972).
HARLOW, V. T., *The Founding of the Second British Empire* (1964).
MORRIS, R. B., *The Peacemakers*, New York (1965).

Chapter 5   Sidelines: The Archdeacon's Family and the Second Sir Henry (1737–1858)

A. *Manuscripts*

Strachey papers, Somerset Record Office, Taunton.
Strachey papers (Sir Richard Strachey), India Office Library.

B. *Printed Material*

BAKER, RUSSELL & STENNING, A. H., *Record of Old Westminsters* (1928).
SOUTHEY, R., *Life and Correspondence*, ed. C. C. Southey (1849).
—— *Selection of the Letters of R. Southey*, ed. J. W. Warter (1856).
—— *New Letters of Robert Southey*, ed. K. Curry, New York and London (1965).
STRACHEY, J. ST LOE, *The Adventure of Living* (1922).

Chapter 6   *'The English Adonis' in Persia: Richard Strachey*
                (1781–1847)

A. *Manuscripts*

Strachey Papers, Somerset Record Office, Taunton.
John Adam Papers, India Office Library and Records.

B. *Printed Material*

CURZON, LORD, *Persia and the Persian Question* (1892).
KAYE, J. W., *The Life of John Malcolm* (1856).
MALCOLM, J., *Sketches of Persia* (1828).

Chapter 7   *With the Kirkpatricks in India: Edward Strachey*
                (1774–1808)

A. *Manuscripts*

Strachey Papers (Sir Richard Strachey), India Office Library and
    Records.
Elphinstone Papers, India Office Library and Records.
The Diary of Mountstuart Elphinstone, India Office Library and
    Records.
Strachey Papers, Somerset Record Office, Taunton.
Papers of Kitty Kirkpatrick's descendants.

B. *Printed Material*

BENCE-JONES, M., *Palaces of the Raj* (1973).
BEVERIDGE, W. H., *India Called Them* (1947).
BRIGGS, H. G., *The Nizam, His History and Relations with the British
    Government* (1861).
BUTLER, I., *The Eldest Brother, the Marquis Wellesley* (1973).
CAMPBELL, A., *Glimpses of the Nizam's Dominions* (1900).
CHAUDHURI, M. R., *An Advanced History of India* (1967).
CHOLESEY, R. D., *Mountstuart Elphinstone* (1971).
COLEBROOKE, T. E., *The life of Mountstuart Elphinstone* (1884).
KAYE, J. W., *The Life of John Malcolm* (1856).
MORNINGTON, LORD, *Letters and Despatches*, ed. Martin
SPEAR, P., *The Nabobs* (1932).
TEMPLE, SIR R., *Journals* (1887).
WELLINGTON, A., *The Despatches of the Duke of Wellington during his
    Campaigns in India*, ed. Lt Col. Gurwood (1834–9).

Chapter 8   London and Thomas Carlyle: Kitty Kirkpatrick
(1808–78)

A. *Manuscripts*

Strachey Papers, India Office Library and Records.
Papers of Kitty Kirkpatrick's descendants.

B. *Printed Material*

CARLYLE, A. ED., *The Love letters of Thomas Carlyle and Jane Welsh* (1909).
CARLYLE, A. ED., *New Letters and memorials of Jane Welsh Carlyle* (1903).
CARLYLE, T., *Reminiscences* (1887).
FROUDE, J. A., *Thomas Carlyle: A History of the First Forty Years of His Life*, (1890 edition).
—— *Thomas Carlyle: A History of his Life in London* (1890 edition).
MERCER, E., 'The Blumine of Sartor Resartus', *Westminster Gazette* CXIII (1894).
POCOCK AND GARNETT, *Caldore and Miscellanea* Preface by Sir E. Strachey (1894).
STRACHEY, SIR E., 'James Mill', *Spectator* (15 April 1882).
STRACHEY, SIR E., 'Some Letters and Conversations of Thomas Carlyle', *Atlantic Monthly* (June 1894).
STRACHEY, G., 'Carlyle and the Rose Goddess', *Nineteenth Century* (Sept 1892).
STRACHEY, G., 'Reminiscences of Carlyle', *New Review* (July 1893).
STRACHEY, H., 'Carlyle's First Love' *Spectator* (9 October 1909).

Chapter 9   The Senior Line: Edward Strachey and his sons
(1812–1927)

A. *Manuscripts*

Strachey Papers, Somerset Record Office, Taunton.

B. *Printed Material*

LEAR, E., *Nonsense Songs and Stories*. Preface by Sir Edward Strachey (1894).
MAURICE, F., *F. D. Maurice* (1884).
STRACHEY, AMY, *John St Loe Strachey and his Paper* (1930).
STRACHEY, SIR E., 'Recollections of F. D. Maurice', *Cornhill Magazine* (April 1897).
STRACHEY, J. ST LOE, *The Adventure of Living* (1922).

Chapter 10   India Again: Henry Strachey and his brothers, William and George (1816–1912)

A. *Manuscripts*

Strachey Papers (Sir Richard Strachey), India Office Library and Records.

B. *Printed Material*

The Geographical Journal (Jan–June 1908; April 1912).
HEDIN, SVEN, 'The Kumaon Glaciers', *Geographical Journal* (August 1910).
Journal of the Royal Geographical Society XIX (1849), XLV (1875).
Proceedings of the Royal Geographical Society XXII (1852), XXIII (1853).
STRACHEY, AMY, *John St Loe Strachey and his Paper* (1930).
STRACHEY, J. ST LOE, *The Adventure of Living* (1922).
WILLIAMS ELLIS, AMABEL, *All Stracheys are Cousins* (1983).
OBIT, 'Col. H. Strachey' *The Times* (10 Feb 1912).

Chapter 11   Servants of India: Richard and John (1817–66)

A. *Manuscripts*

Strachey Papers (Sir Richard Strachey), India Office Library and Records.
Unpublished Memoirs of Lady Strachey, Strachey Trust Papers.

B. *Printed Material*

Journal of the Royal Geographical Society XXI (1851).
Journal of the Linnaean Society XXX (1902).
LAURIE, W. F. B., *Sketches of Some Distinguished Anglo-Indians* (1887–8).
MOORHOUSE, G., *India Britannica* (1983).
OBITS. Sir Richard Strachey *The Times* (13 Feb. 1908).
    Sir John Strachey *The Times* (20 Dec. 1907)
    Journal of the Royal Engineers (May 1908).
    Nature (by W. N. Shaw) LXXVII (27 Feb. 1908).
    Popular Science (April 1908).
    Sir Richard Strachey, *The Spectator*, (22 Feb. 1908) (by C. A. Elliott).
    Sir John Strachey, *The Spectator* (28 Dec. 1907).

Chapter 12 The Strachey Raj: Richard and John (1866–1908)

A. *Manuscripts*

Strachey Papers (Sir Richard Strachey), India Office Library and Records.
Unpublished Memoirs of Lady Strachey, Strachey Trust Papers.

B. *Printed Material*

BENCE-JONES, M., *Palaces of the Raj* (1973).
HUDDLESTONE, W., *The History of the East India Railway* (1906).
LUTYENS, M., *The Lyttons in India* (1979).
SETON-KERR, W. S., *Grant of Rothiemurcus* (1899).
STRACHEY, SIR JOHN, *India: Its Administration and Progress* (4th edition 1911, originally entitled *The Finances and Public Works of India* 1882).
—— *Hastings and the Rohilla War* (1892).

Chapter 13 Richard: A Long Career (1817–1908)

A. *Manuscripts*

Strachey Papers (Sir Richard Strachey), India Office Library and Records.
Unpublished Memoirs of Lady Strachey, Strachey Trust Papers.

B. *Printed Material*

OBITS, See Chapter 11.

Chapter 14 'Dearest Cat': Richard's Wife Janie (1840–1928)

A. *Manuscripts*

Strachey Papers (Sir Richard Strachey), India Office Library and Records.
Unpublished Memoirs of Lady Strachey, Strachey Trust Papers.

B. *Printed Material*

ASKWITH, B., *Two Victorian Families* (1971).
FRENCH BOYD, E., *Bloomsbury Heritage* (1976).

Index

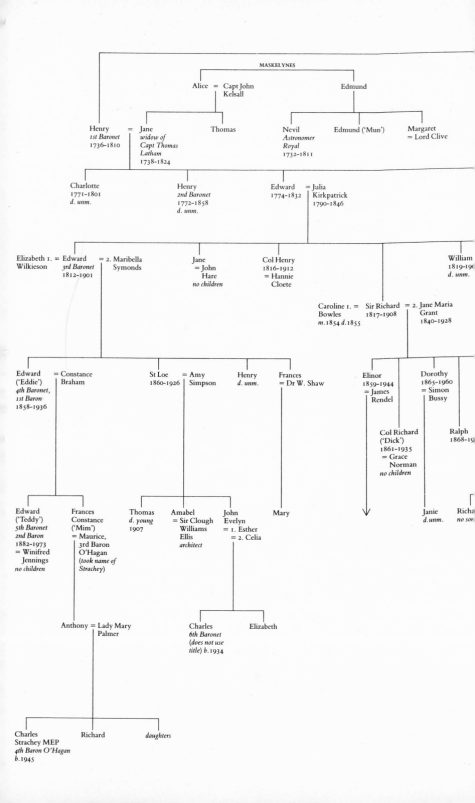

MASKELYNES

Alice = Capt John Kelsall

Edmund

Henry *1st Baronet* 1736–1810 = Jane *widow of Capt Thomas Latham* 1738–1824

Thomas

Nevil *Astronomer Royal* 1732–1811

Edmund ('Mun')

Margaret = Lord Clive

Charlotte 1771–1801 *d. unm.*

Henry *2nd Baronet* 1772–1858 *d. unm.*

Edward 1774–1832 = Julia Kirkpatrick 1790–1846

Elizabeth 1. = Edward *3rd Baronet* 1812–1901 = 2. Maribella Symonds
Wilkieson

Jane = John Hare *no children*

Col Henry 1816–1912 = Hannie Cloete

William 1819–19.. *d. unm.*

Caroline 1. = Sir Richard Bowles *m.1854 d.1855* 1817–1908 = 2. Jane Maria Grant 1840–1928

Edward ('Eddie') *4th Baronet, 1st Baron* 1858–1936 = Constance Braham

St Loe 1860–1926 = Amy Simpson

Henry *d. unm.*

Frances = Dr W. Shaw

Elinor 1859–1944 = James Rendel

Dorothy 1865–1960 = Simon Bussy

Ralph 1868–19..

Col Richard ('Dick') 1861–1935 = Grace Norman *no children*

Edward ('Teddy') *5th Baronet 2nd Baron* 1882–1973 = Winifred Jennings *no children*

Frances Constance ('Mim') = Maurice, *3rd Baron O'Hagan* (took name of Strachey)

Thomas *d. young* 1907

Amabel = Sir Clough Williams Ellis *architect*

John Evelyn = 1. Esther = 2. Celia

Mary

Janie *d.unm.*

Richa.. *no so..*

Anthony = Lady Mary Palmer

Charles *6th Baronet* (*does not use title*) *b.1934*

Elizabeth

Charles Strachey MEP *4th Baron O'Hagan* *b.1945*

Richard

daughters